CHICANOS IN CALIFORNIA

CHICANOS IN CALIFORNIA

A History of Mexican Americans in California

Albert Camarillo

series editors:
Norris Hundley, jr.
John A. Schutz

Materials For Today's Learning, Inc.
Sparks, Nevada

CHICANOS IN CALIFORNIA:
A HISTORY OF MEXICAN AMERICANS IN CALIFORNIA
Albert Camarillo

© Copyright 1990 by Materials For Today's Learning, Inc.
1575 Linda Way, Sparks, Nevada 89431
All rights reserved.

Manufactured in the United States of America

Library of Congress catalog card number: 84-14475

ISBN 0-929651-08-1

9 · 9 8 7

EDITORS' INTRODUCTION

MENTION THE NAME CALIFORNIA and the popular mind conjures up images of romance and adventure of the sort that prompted the Spaniards in the 1540s to name the locale after a legendary Amazon queen. State of mind no less than geographic entity, California has become a popular image of a wonderful land of easy wealth, good health, pleasant living, and unlimited opportunities. While this has been true for some, for others it has been a land of disillusionment, and for too many it has become a place of crowded cities, congested roadways, smog, noise, racial unrest, and other problems. Still, the romantic image has persisted to make California the most populated state in the Union and the home of more newcomers each year than came during the first three hundred years following discovery by Europeans.

For most of its history California has been shrouded in mystery, better known for its terrain than for its settlers—first the Indians who arrived at least 11,000 years ago and then the Spaniards who followed in 1769. Spaniards, Mexicans, and blacks added only slightly to the non-Indian population until the American conquest of 1846 ushered in an era of unparalleled growth. With the discovery of gold, the building of the transcontinental railroad, and the development of crops and cities, people in massive numbers from all parts of the world began to inhabit the region. Thus California became a land of newcomers where a rich mixture of cultures pervades.

Fact and fiction are intertwined so well into the state's traditions and folklore that they are sometimes difficult to separate. But close scrutiny reveals that the people of California have made many solid contributions in land and water use, conservation of resources, politics, education, transportation, labor organization, literature, architectural styles, and learning to live with people of different cultural and ethnic heritages. These contributions, as well as those instances when Californians performed less admirably, are woven into the design of the Golden State Series. The volumes in the Series are meant to be suggestive rather than exhaustive, interpretive rather than definitive. They invite the general public, the student, the scholar, and the teacher to read them not only for digested materials from a wide range of recent scholarship, but also for some new insights and ways of perceiving old problems. The Series, we trust, will be only the beginning of each reader's inquiry into the past of a state rich in historical excitement and significant in its impact on the nation.

Norris Hundley, jr.
John A. Schutz

CONTENTS

For Susan
with love

PREFACE

SOMETIME IN THE twenty-first century, according to population projections for California, people of Mexican descent
will outnumber all other residents in the state. This projection
assumes, of course, that Mexicans will not lose their identity in
the sea of other inhabitants who have been drawing new cultures into the old since the establishment of the British colonies.
If the Mexicans in California should become the majority, they
will have come nearly full circle from the 1840s when an influx
of newcomers from the eastern United States and elsewhere
first reduced them from majority to minority status in this
land. Their roots thus are deep in the past of California and the
Southwest, and an understanding of their historical experiences is essential to an understanding of modern California
society. Regrettably, most Californians, Mexicans as well as
non-Mexicans, know little about the state's Mexican heritage
beyond what they have read in their school texts about the
"Spanish Dons," the missions, and the ranchos of the late eigh-
teenth and early nineteenth centuries. They know even less
about California Hispanic peoples during the years between the
U.S.–Mexican War of 1846–1848 and the 1980s. In the past
decade, however, scholars have uncovered a wealth of information about Mexican Americans and have changed traditional
views of Chicanos as a "forgotten people" with a "lost history."

But attitudes die slowly. A cover story in *Time* magazine
solemnly announced in 1978 that "as America's latest great
wave of immigrants, Hispanics are learning another hard lesson:
latecomers start at the bottom." Though newcomers continue to
make up a portion of the Mexican community in the state,
California's Hispanic past stretches back more than two centuries, while in other parts of the Southwest the heritage is
nearly four hundred years old. The history of Chicanos in California can be traced to the settlements of missionaries, soldiers,

and civilian colonists and the emergence of a *mestizo* society which has struggled to maintain its ethnic-cultural identity since American rule and the tidal wave of newcomers. Chicano history is the saga of a diverse people collectively experiencing being Mexican in an Anglo environment. This experience has included recurrent immigration from Mexico, political resistance, urbanization and barrioization, sociocultural continuity and change, adjustment and assimilation into American society, racial and social class stratification, labor conflicts, and economic stagnation and progress. These and other themes characterize the history of Californians of Mexican descent, but they also constitute an inextricable part of the history of all Californians. In addition, they shed light on the experiences of Mexicans everywhere in the U.S. Though the record of Mexicans in California has elements that set it apart from the history of Mexicans in other locales, the similarities are more striking than the differences. Thus this book forms part of the larger national history of the second-largest and fastest-growing minority in the country.

Persons of Mexican origin in California and elsewhere in the U.S. are a heterogeneous people who may trace their heritage back to Indian, black, and Spanish influences and who may come from various areas of Mexico and the American Southwest. Their diversity is aptly illustrated by the many terms used to identify them: Latino, Latin American, Mexican American, Spanish speaking, Mexicano, Raza, Chicano, Hispanic, and others. These terms say as much about internal differences as about how the larger society has viewed this ethnic population over time. Historically, Mexican (and Mexicano) is the term with which most members of the group have identified themselves. More recently, three other designations have been commonly used: Mexican American, Hispanic, and Chicano. Mexican American is widely accepted by second- or third-generation persons of immigrant stock, while Hispanic — a new term which by definition incorporates the other U.S. Spanish-origin subgroups — is used perhaps more frequently by the general public than by the group members themselves. The origin of the word Chicano (aside from those highly suspect hypotheses which suggest that the term derives from the Aztec period) dates from the late nineteenth and early twentieth centuries when it was used as a self-referent by the working-class Mexican immigrants in some, but not all, southwestern barrios. Chicano is an emotional term, one that may infuriate some people, mostly of the older generation, who perceive it as a derogatory, politicized word used by militants and activists. To a younger generation of adolescents and college students, the word, which gained its greatest popularity following the civil rights movement of the 1960s, expresses a cultural and ethnic pride as well as a social, political, and historical awareness of being Mexican in the U.S. It connotes a common link among people of Mexican origins in the U.S. who share elements of religion, culture, language, and mestizo heritage. Since no one term has gained universal acceptance, this book uses Mexican, Mexican American, and Chicano interchangeably. When necessary, the distinction between the native and foreign-born is presented. The appellation used to refer to non-Mexican, Caucasian people is Anglo American or Anglo, a term applied by most scholars to non-Hispanic Americans of European descent.

California is a multiracial and multiethnic society, with its many Asians, blacks, American Indians, and whites of various European backgrounds. Interwoven into the state's multiethnic past is the important role that Mexicans have played in the evolution of California's diversity. This book profiles the history of what is currently the state's largest minority group, especially the ways in which the group has shaped the California past and the ways in which the dominant society, in turn, has influenced the lives of Mexican Americans.

*

Numerous colleagues have contributed ideas which are synthesized in this book. But I am especially indebted to Antonia Castañeda, Pedro Castillo, and Carlos E. Cortés, good friends who reviewed a draft of the entire manuscript. I am also grateful to Anna Tower who typed the final version of the manuscript during my fellowship year at the Center for Advanced Study in the Behavioral Sciences. My fellowship there was supported by grants from the Rockefeller Foundation and the Andrew S. Mellon Foundation.

I have been most fortunate over the past ten years to have such a fine friend and editor as Norris Hundley. My first two books owe much to his pen and insightful editorial comments. I also want to thank my other editor, John Schutz, for his incisive remarks and help in editing the manuscript.

This book is dedicated to Ernesto Galarza, a friend and colleague. As activist-scholar, he was an inspiration and model for me and other Chicanos.

A.C.

Stanford
July 1984

CHAPTER ONE

The Foundations of Mexican California: 1769-1848

T HE MIGRATION OF PEOPLE from the interior of Mexico to
what is now the American Southwest began nearly four
hundred years ago. With the establishment of the first Spanish
colonial settlement in Santa Fe, New Mexico, in 1610, the far
northern frontier of Mexico remained a continuing attraction to
new settlers. Though sparsely inhabited, the borderlands gradually expanded into southern Texas, Arizona, and finally into the
coastal strip of California.

The men and women pioneers who settled in California, like
their counterparts elsewhere on the northern frontier, were a
mestizo people primarily of Spanish and Indian descent, but
often of African ancestry as well. Though peninsular Spaniards
and *criollos* (Spaniards born in the New World) were among
them, most frontier settlers were of mixed blood and culture.
The process of *mestizaje*—the making of a society of mestizo
people—had begun with the earliest Spanish settlements in
Mexico (known as New Spain until 1821), and by the time
the colonization of California began in 1769, the process was
well advanced. For these latest of newcomers Alta, or upper,

California represented the final effort in the colonization of the northern borderlands. Spain's hegemony lasted only half a century before Mexico won its independence in 1821. The Mexican Republican period was of even shorter duration, ending in 1847, when the province surrendered to the U.S. during the Mexican War. In the previous three-quarters of a century, however, Spanish and Mexican foundations of society and culture in California were well laid.

Spanish Colonial California (1769–1821)

SPAIN GAINED A FIRM FOOTHOLD in Alta California by utilizing colonizing tactics that were centuries old. Those tactics relied on three principal institutions—the mission, the presidio, and the pueblo. The earliest missions, the first founded in 1769 in San Diego, experienced a precarious two decades in Alta California, but in the 1790s they had become self-sufficient communities which served basically two functions: christianizing local Indians and providing an economic base for the northern coastal frontier. The other two frontier institutions, though initially less influential in shaping society, nevertheless played important roles. The *presidio* (fort), never really a bastion of strength in the province, provided defense for the missions and the *pueblos,* the first of which were San Jose and Los Angeles. They were secular towns inhabited by *pobladores* or recruited civilian settlers—families as well as individuals—and by retired soldiers and their families. Much of the early conflict in Alta California resulted from clashes among the personnel who administered the colonial institutions: the Franciscan friars often quarreling with the presidial soldiers because of their undesirable influences on mission neophyte Indians; the secular administrators frequently criticizing the missionaries out of jealousy of their power and influence; and the presidio officers objecting to the encroaching jurisdictions of both church and pueblo, particularly as the garrisons became ill equipped and undermanned during the final years of Spanish rule.[1]

From the beginning California's colonial society was heterogeneous. The small but growing population (approximately 900 in 1790, 2,000 in 1810, and about 3,500 by the end of the Spanish era) consisted of Spaniards, mestizos, mulattos, and Indian colonists from the interior of New Spain. The intermarriage of presidio soldiers and settlers with native California Indians added to the racial and cultural diversity of early frontier society. Those of mixed blood were numerically dominant, but those who exercised political, social, and economic control were the Spanish peninsulares and criollos—colonial administrators, military officers, and Franciscans.

The stereotypic image of peaceful, somnolent, and romantic "Spanish" California—appropriately labeled the "fantasy heritage" by Carey McWilliams—beclouds the diversity and rivalry among social classes and races.[2] For nearly every story of strong relationships between benevolent mission priests and Indian neophytes, there are tales of missionary maltreatment which fostered Indian revolts, such as those in 1824 that occurred at Santa Barbara, Purísima, Concepción, and Santa Inez missions. For every romantic legend of wealthy Spanish dons, there are the hard realities of frontier life that confronted presidio soldiers and pueblo settlers alike. California society was, thus, an amalgam of races, social classes, institutions, and living conditions.

The most common characteristic of Alta California society during the Spanish colonial period was the shared experiences of life in an isolated, frontier post. The far northern frontier was too remote to be included in the social and cultural mainstream of interior New Spain. Though some individuals with resources and connections traveled to Mexico City and elsewhere in the empire, most settlers seldom ventured beyond the boundaries of the province. Even contacts with other borderland settlements, such as the more numerous New Mexico outposts, were rare. Except for the infrequent visits of supply ships and trading vessels and the even more infrequent overland caravans from central Mexico, California remained an isolated area on the edge of the frontier. This isolation bred in California and in other borderland settlements a regional parochialism in which residents identified far more with their provinces than with central Mexico or Spain. These regional identities were reinforced during the subsequent Mexican Republican period.[3]

Southern view of "Mexican Camp," New Almaden mercury mines located about 14 miles from the city of San Jose, circa 1890. (*Courtesy of New Almaden Mercury Mining Museum*)

Mexican National Period (1822–1846)

THE NEWS OF MEXICO'S achievement of independence from Spain in 1821 caused little fanfare among Alta Californianos. There were, of course, the expected apprehensions expressed by the Spanish-born governor Pablo Vicente de Solá and some of his soldiers, but their fears soon dissipated. By the 1830s, however, Mexico's concerns with republicanism and constitutionalism had developed into serious political issues which eventually altered the relationship between church and state as well as the nature of social classes in the California province.

The major change that affected nearly all sectors of society was secularization of the missions. Though independent Mexico decided early to dismantle the missions, the actual process of secularization did not begin in earnest until after 1833. Spain's original intent had been to transform the missions gradually into local parishes and secular settlements, distribute mission lands to the ex-neophytes, and assimilate the Indians into nearby civilian towns. In theory, but not in practice, the Mexican government intended secularization to work much as the Spanish had originally conceived. The proclamation by California governor José Figueroa in 1834 called for a systematic distribution of half of the missions' real estate to the Indians. The other half of church property was to be administered by secular agents of the province with the intent of continuing livestock grazing and agriculture on those lands. According to the terms of the proclamation, the Indians could not sell their newly acquired property, and though they were technically freed from their neophyte status, they were forced by *mayordomos* (managers) to work the land and care for livestock.

The early death of Governor Figueroa and the ensuing period of political instability in the province disrupted governmental supervision of secularization and opened the door to many abuses. Between 1834 and 1846 California mission property, with the sole exception of the lands of mission Santa Barbara, was so unscrupulously administered that few Indians benefited. Some Indians added to the destruction of the missions by plundering and then fleeing from what had become for them a detested institution. Most of the land fell into the private ownership of a relatively few influential families. Though many mestizo ex-soldiers from the dismantled and decaying presidios received modest grants of land in recognition of their military services, the majority of mission holdings went to those families which already held power and influence in California society—such as the Vallejos, De la Guerras, Castros, Picos, Alvarados, and Pachecos.[4]

Though secularization changed the basis of land tenure, it did not alter the pastoral economy. Rather, the transfer of mission lands to private ownership ushered in what has been romantically referred to as the "golden age of the ranchos." The rancho cattle industry, the hide and tallow trade with American and other foreign companies, and subsistence agriculture expanded during the late Mexican period. Between 1830 and 1846 some eight million acres were granted to over eight hundred grantees. Contrary to popular belief, the "Spanish" land grants were mainly products of the Mexican period. Spain's earlier, conservative policy of granting individual tracts had resulted in less than thirty grants, and even then individuals never possessed absolute title, something the king of Spain always held.[5]

The rise of the ranchos in Mexican pastoral California constituted only one of several related societal changes affected directly or indirectly by secularization. The decline of the influence of the Franciscans ushered in a period when individuals vied not only for private property but for political power as well. Under colonial Spain, pobladores had little to say about self-government at the local or provincial level. Outsiders had usually been appointed by distant colonial viceroys or by other powerful administrators in Mexico City or Spain. Though self-government increased during the final decade of Spain's rule in Mexico, autonomous local politics and provincial representation was a product of Mexican republicanism. The federal constitution of 1824 allowed for far more regional self-government than had existed under Spain, and local government—though it existed technically during the colonial period—blossomed in the new republic. Due to internal political problems in Mexico, however, there were no clear guidelines for the administration of the far northern territories and, consequently, the borderlands had less autonomy than the central states of Mexico. Neverthe-less, local municipalities were governed by *ayuntamientos,* or town councils of elected representatives, and each province had its *diputación,* a legislature also composed of elected officials. Republicanism in the new Mexican provinces thus opened ave-nues for the political aspirant.

Republicanism was also accompanied by political instability in California. Competition among rival *políticos,* disagree-ments over provincial autonomy within the Republic, differ-ences about separation of church and state, rivalry between northern and southern residents of the province, and discord over administration of secularized mission landholdings all con-tributed to political unrest. Governors, it seemed, changed as often as the seasons. Political infighting among various indi-viduals and among leading native Californian families ofttimes caused as much controversy as did the appointment of a non-Californian as governor by the central government in Mexico City. Though the disharmony during the 1830s and 1840s was intense, it rarely resulted in open warfare.

The changes that a new form of government and seculariza-tion wrought in California were clearly visible in social and class differences. The elite of society, both on the ranchos and in the pueblos, were a small group of influential and wealthy ranchero families who controlled the government, the pastoral economy, and the "culture." These self-proclaimed "Spaniards" —though most were mestizos—constituted between five and ten percent of the total non-Indian population, which numbered approximately 6,000 at the start of the Mexican-American War. The large majority of the mestizo population resided in coastal towns and on nearby ranchos. Some owned small land grants and carried on subsistence farming and grazing. Women were central to this local family economy, both as tillers of the soil and as tenders of livestock. Others, nearly all men, worked in skilled pastoral trades as *vaqueros* or cowboys, saddlemakers, silversmiths, and blacksmiths. Most settlers lived in the pueblos of Los Angeles, San Diego, Santa Barbara, Monterey, Santa Cruz, and San Jose, where they owned small private lots on which they built adobe homes and grazed and farmed the adja-cent *ejido* (public land) granted to all pueblo residents. The pobladores also worked on a seasonal basis during the *rodeos* and *matanzas* (roundups and slaughters) on the ranchos. At the bottom of society in Mexican California were the former mission Indians (about 15,000 ex-neophytes in 1834). Some congregated in small villages or *rancherías*, on the ranchos as laborers, or in the pueblos as servants for wealthy ranchero families; others returned to isolated Indian communities in the mountains or deserts.[6]

Within the social classes of Mexican California existed another division based on gender. Since the early decades of Spanish colonization, and increasingly during the Mexican period, women on the far northern frontier assumed critical roles in society, both as workers in the pastoral economy and as keystones of the family unit. Life for women was difficult and entailed many hardships and multiple responsibilities. Though women of the wealthier ranchero class performed less hard labor than the other women, they were responsible for overseeing the traditional domestic duties of cooking, cleaning, and entertaining guests. During the years when their families were turning their small land grants into prosperous ranchos, the lives of these women were more akin to the experiences of the large majority of women in the province. In addition to work in subsistence rancho and pueblo agriculture and livestock production, some women earned wages or room and board as washerwomen, midwives, seamstresses, and teachers. Women were also commonly the *curanderas* or folk healers knowledgeable about the use of herbs and other medicinal treatments. Outside of domestic chores that fell to women and children, clearly defined sexual divisions of labor did not prevail. Women worked alongside men in the fields and pastures in a collective environment which required all family members to contribute food to the household.[7]

The lives of women in Mexican California differed sharply from the stereotypic views found in the literature written by American visitors to the province. Yankees in California, like their counterparts writing about women in other areas of the borderlands, portrayed Mexican females in contradictory ways. Upper-class "Spanish ladies" were described as virtuous, gracious hostesses, with fair complexions like those of women in the United States. Most lower-class women, however, were depicted as immoral and attractive to American sailors from trading vessels because of their winning smiles, dark good looks, and exotic dancing. The one characteristic about which American commentators agreed was the beauty of Mexican women.[8]

The literature on Mexican women during the mid-1800s also portrayed their unequal treatment by men. Hispanic traditions from Europe were male-centered and received reinforcement in central Mexico and on the frontier. Men were patriarchs who controlled the secular and religious institutions and dominated the households and extended families. Yet Hispanic traditions also afforded women community property rights and entitlement to retain separately any property they possessed prior to marriage.

Though Mexican California was characterized by social divisions based on gender, race, class, and culture, some aspects of provincial life softened these divisions and promoted social unity. For example, avenues of social and occupational mobility were available to the mestizo population. Mestizo soldiers as well as civilian settlers often acquired land grants for services rendered to the republic. Many others remained as laborers and skilled workers in the pastoral and related pueblo economy which provided access to communal pueblo lands for subsistence gardening and livestock grazing. Also fostering cooperation among the classes was the isolation of frontier California. Families and individuals had to rely on one another for support rather than on the rudimentary territorial government or the distant capital of the republic. Few ever lacked food, shelter, or other basic needs. In addition, the paternalistic system of godparent relationships — *compadrazgo* — provided economic, social, and religious bonds among wealthy families and those in the working class. *Padrinos* and *madrinas* (godfathers and godmothers) took their responsibilities seriously, thus encouraging a social cohesiveness through a system of respect and patronage. Extended family networks, enlarged through compadrazgo and nurtured by a family-oriented economy, ensured the centrality and strength of the family unit in frontier society. Language, religion, and common cultural mores also contributed to softening class lines in California society.

Views of American Foreigners

SOME EARLY YANKEE VISITORS to Mexican California recorded their experiences and their impressions of the local populace. Among the best-known commentators were Richard Henry Dana, who recounted a sojourn in 1835–1836 in his famous *Two Years Before the Mast,* and Alfred Robinson, a New England trader who first came to California in 1829 and later married into the prominent De La Guerra family.

"The Californians are an idle, thriftless people," wrote Dana, "and can make nothing for themselves." "The men are thriftless, proud, extravagant, and very much given to gaming," he added, "and the women have but little education but a good deal of beauty, and their morality, of course, is none of the best." "In the hands of an enterprising people, what a country this might be!" he concluded. Similarly, Robinson described the men of San Jose as "generally indolent, and addicted to many vices, caring little for the welfare of their children, who, like themselves, grow up unworthy members of society." Dana and Robinson provided readers in the U.S. with some of the first accounts, most of them negative, of the land and people of California. Such attitudes towards Spain had existed for decades in the U.S. and for centuries in England. They derived primarily from anti-Catholic sentiments and the so-called "Black Legend" (the characterization of the Spanish as plunderers of Indian civilizations who allegedly differed from the English colonists with their desire to establish new lives in the New World). Mexicans, because of their Spanish origins, fell heir to these prejudices as well as the stigma of being a racially mixed, inferior people. The popularity of accounts like those of Dana and Robinson influenced the opinions of other Americans who came to California during the 1840s and 1850s with preconceived views of the Mexicans of California and other borderland areas as "lazy, ignorant, bigoted, superstitious, cheating, thieving, gambling, cruel, sinister, cowardly half-breeds."[9]

Though many American visitors portrayed the Mexicans in a negative light, some newcomers opted to remain in California and assimilate into Mexican society through marriage, conversion to Catholicism, and naturalization. By the mid-1840s, however, the so-called "Mexicanized gringos" were becoming an anomaly as newer American immigrants caught up in the craze of Manifest Destiny began arriving. Settling mostly in northern California and away from Mexican settlements, these militant critics of the society had no intention of assimilating and symbolized real portents of change in the province. They precipitated the Bear Flag Revolt in 1846 which embittered relations for decades.[10]

Bear Flag Revolt, War, and Annexation

AS INTEREST IN CALIFORNIA grew during the 1840s, so did the desire of the United States to acquire Mexico's far northern territory. Long coveted for its strategic military location and fine natural harbors on the Pacific, California became a primary target for annexation in the plans of newly elected president James K. Polk in 1845. Whether he conspired to take California by using local residents is not certain, but Polk wanted to acquire California in whatever way might be necessary. When viewed in this light, the short-lived Bear Flag Revolt encouraged by John C. Frémont and his band of cohorts in the Sonoma-Sacramento area seems unnecessary. The independent republic of California that it created gave way almost immediately to U.S. authority. In the interim, however, the Bear Flaggers managed to flame racial hatred by their capture and ill treatment of a highly respected rancher, military commandant Mariano Vallejo, and their slaughter of other Mexicans in the north.[11]

The outcome of the Mexican War was decided largely by military action in central Mexico, but the California campaign ensured the U.S. the most prized territory. Spearheading the war effort on the Pacific Coast were naval forces which moved upon Monterey, the tiny capital of the province, and proclaimed the occupation of California. The naval forces, together with volunteers, many of whom were former Bear Flaggers, then secured the southern part of the province. A small army of occupation went to Los Angeles and took control. But Mexican resistance developed as news of the atrocities against northern countrymen by Bear Flaggers reached pueblos in the south and as American military leaders took repressive actions, particularly in Los Angeles. The Mexicans retaliated by driving the American detachment from Los Angeles and taking control of the southern half of the province. U.S. naval forces then fought skirmishes with Mexicans and forced their retreat once again. The end of Mexican military resistance came when the then-Colonel Frémont marched south with three hundred men and General Stephen Kearny arrived with some troops from New Mexico. The only major battle of the war fought in California involved Kearny's tired troops, who were confronted by a group of mounted lancers at San Pasqual. The skirmish took place near present-day Escondido and resulted in a few casualties. A little later, the poorly armed Mexicans were unable to mount sufficient military strength to forestall the capitulation of Los Angeles when Frémont and Kearny converged on the area and received the Mexican surrender in January 1847.[12]

Just over a year later, in 1848, the signing of the Treaty of Guadalupe Hidalgo formally ended the war and provided for the annexation of California and other territories of the new American Southwest to the U.S. The cost of the war to Mexico was dear—nearly half its national domain, including Texas, which had earlier rebelled against Mexico. According to terms of the treaty, the Mexican population of about 6,000 had one year to relocate in Mexico or remain and become U.S. citizens.[13]

A false sense of security for Mexicans in California came with the end of the war and assurances from American military and civilian personnel that property rights would be respected. The peace treaty also made vague references to property, religious, and civil rights. During 1848 it had appeared to most Mexicans that the change in sovereignty had not altered the nature of their society. However, by 1850 the rise of a new American social order—spurred unexpectedly by the discovery of gold—had begun to transform their lives and the world they had known.

CHAPTER TWO

From "Mexican" to "American" California: 1848–1900

F OR ANGLO AMERICANS, the era following the annexation of California was one of tremendous economic growth and population increase. The newcomers also quickly established their own political and social institutions and looked forward eagerly and confidently to California's future. By 1900 the state had become tied by railroads and trade into the economy of the nation and had long completed its transition from Mexican province to American state. The population had risen to 1,500,000.

In the half century following annexation, California's Mexican people experienced changes altogether different from those encountered by their Anglo counterparts. Instead of confidence about their future, most felt overwhelmed by the surge of new people into their homeland. While Anglo Americans achieved remarkable economic growth, Mexicans suffered dramatic economic decline; while Americans acquired political control and stability, Mexicans became politically powerless; while Americans established their cultural and social system, Mexicans struggled to retain what they could of their traditional life styles. The transition from Mexican to American California was a period of traumatic change for Spanish-speaking peoples compelled to grapple with their new "Mexican American" reality.

Conflict in the North: 1850s

T HE DISCOVERY OF GOLD IN 1848 destroyed whatever possibility existed for a smooth transition from a Mexican to an American territory. The gold rush immediately flung California into the national and international spotlight and attracted a massive number of Americans and foreigners in search of wealth. Those who sought their fortunes in forms other than gold fixed their eyes soon on the land and trade. Farmers and ranchers joined with merchants to serve the exploding population in the towns and cities. California became an American state in 1850, just two years after the Treaty of Guadalupe Hidalgo.

Practically overnight the demographic profile of the state also changed. In the north the Mexican majority became the minority within months after James Marshall's gold find at Sutter's mill. The Mexican population in the territory, which increased to about 8,000 in 1849 due to the influx of miners from Sonora, Mexico, was small compared to the virtual human tidal wave of 100,000 "forty-niners" who descended on California and who were followed by greater numbers of migrants in the 1850s. Though California Mexicans were among the earliest in the Mother Lode, they were soon systematically driven from the diggings. At first Anglos considered the native Californians "foreigners" and "greasers," and harassed and assaulted many of them. Later, as large numbers of Sonoran Mexicans, Chileans, Chinese, and other foreigners came to the gold fields, Americans struck out at them with discriminatory legislation such as the Foreign Miners' Tax. Violence effectively drove the California and Sonora Mexicans away. Thousands of the Sonorans (estimated between 5,000 and 10,000 in the early 1850s), many of whom had traveled with their families, returned home; others migrated along with the native Californians to the old pueblos, particularly San Jose, Santa Barbara, and Los Angeles.

The racial and economic discrimination against Mexicans that first manifested itself in the Sierra Nevada gold diggings soon became endemic throughout the state. In the north hundreds of unsuccessful American miners focused attention on the "undeveloped" land that surrounded them and soon these squatters were occupying large areas encompassed by Mexican land grants. Beleaguered by trespassers and denied protection by authorities, the Mexican landowners were defenseless against the onslaught. To make matters worse, the California Land Law of 1851 challenged the validity of Spanish and Mexican land grants. The legislation, enacted by Congress at the urging of U.S. Senator William Gwin of California, established a Board of Land Commissioners in San Francisco to examine the titles of some fourteen million acres of land granted under Spanish and Mexican law. Those grants, if found invalid, would become part of the public domain and could be sold to individuals. Though the Treaty of Guadalupe Hidalgo guaranteed Mexicans "the enjoyment of all the rights of the United States according to the principles of the Constitution and . . . the free enjoyment of their liberty and property," its vagueness as to property claims offered little protection to the land grantees. Reacting to the Land Board's rejection of some well-known Mexican land grants, ranchero Juan Bandini of southern California complained:

> Of the lands mentioned, some have ˙ en in the quiet possession of the proprietors and their famiı ᵤs for forty or fifty years. On them they have reared themselves homes — they have enclosed and cultivated fields — there they and their children were born — and there they lived in peace and comparative plenty. But now, our inheritance is turned to strangers — our houses to aliens. We have drunken our water for money — our wood is sold unto us. Our necks are under persecution — we labor and have no rest.[1]

"Viewed from any angle, the results of the federal law were unsatisfactory," concluded historian Robert C. Cleland. "In actual practice it violated the spirit of the Treaty of Guadalupe Hidalgo . . . and did irreparable injury to a great body of legitimate landowners, caused an endless amount of confusion and litigation, and seriously interfered with the economic progress of the state for almost a generation."[2]

In less than a decade, most Mexicans in the north had lost

their lands. Typical was the experience of the Peralta family, owners of Rancho San Antonio—the site of present-day Oakland. They lost everything when squatters cut down their fruit trees, killed their cattle, destroyed their buildings, and even fenced off the roads leading to the rancho. Especially insidious were the actions of attorney Horace Carpentier, who tricked Vicente Peralta into signing a "lease" which turned out to be a mortgage against the 19,000-acre rancho. The lands became Carpentier's when Peralta refused to repay the loan he believed was fraudulently incurred. The Peraltas had no choice but to abandon the homesite they had occupied for two generations. The Berreyesa family of San Jose experienced an equally tragic loss. Nicolás Berreyesa, driven nearly insane by the murder of his brother and two nephews at the hands of Americans during the Bear Flag Revolt and by squatters occupying his land, unwarily took the advice of James Jake, an unscrupulous American newcomer. Jake assured the ranchero that the only way to retain his land was to claim squatter's rights. After surveying plots for Berreyesa family members, Jake then claimed the remaining land—the bulk of the estate—for himself. Berreyesa lost the subsequent court fight to reclaim his property. Other relatives lost their lives defending claims, but the survivors did not lose hope of a favorable court ruling until 1876, when the U.S. Supreme Court upheld prior decisions against the Californios. Historian Leonard Pitt assessed the outcome for the Berreyesas:

> The seventy members of the once-powerful Berreyesa family, now completely landless and penniless, threw themselves on the mercy of the San Jose town government and begged some small plot as a homesite. Concluding the saddest saga of all, Antonio Berreyesa estimated that of all the old families, his was the "one which most justly complained of the bad faith of the adventurers and squatters and of the treachery of American lawyers."[3]

The combined effects of costly litigation, squatter violence and land occupation, usurious interest rates on loans, unscrupulous attorneys, and tax-delinquent foreclosures separated most Mexican landowners in the northern half of the state from their property.

The loss of land and the influx of Americans during the

1850s soon obscured the Mexican way of life, especially in the north. The small pueblo near Mission Dolores in San Francisco was overrun almost immediately while the pueblos of San Jose, Santa Cruz, and Monterey were also quickly inundated by Anglo newcomers. Racial violence became commonplace everywhere, highlighted by lynchings and mob actions. This changing environment helped foster deep-seated racial animosity and provided the backdrop to the activities of the legendary California bandits Joaquín Murieta and Tiburcio Vásquez.

The notorious Joaquín perhaps best symbolized Mexican-Anglo race relations in California during the 1850s. Shrouded in as much myth as reality, Murieta came from Sonora during the gold rush and soon tangled with Americans because of their treatment of Mexicans. According to some accounts, he sought revenge against all "gringos" after the murder of his wife by miners. Though several Murietas may have existed — simultaneous sightings of Joaquín up and down the state were reported during the early 1850s — the legends portray a man unjustly treated and determined to rob and kill as a way to strike back at the "Americanos." Among Anglos in northern California, especially in Calaveras County, the name Joaquín caused fear and cries for eradication of the "Mexican criminal element," a label applied to a growing number of Mexicans in the state.[4] The exploits of Murieta were a source of special pride to the Spanish-speaking people, for he was among only a handful of Mexicans who refused to submit to Anglo authority in California.

Tiburcio Vásquez, the last of the so-called Mexican "bandidos," also became a popular symbol of resistance to Anglos. A native Californian from a land-owning family in Monterey, he, too, after several run-ins with Americans, embarked on a life of crime and revenge. His activities landed him in San Quentin prison, and after his release he was hounded by authorities and resorted again to robbing Americans of cash and cattle. During the early 1870s he became infamous through some daring stagecoach and other robberies in northern California for which he was pursued by a large posse that tracked him 2,000 miles. The posse finally surrounded him in a ranch house north of Los Angeles in an area now called Vásquez Rocks. Tiburcio was wounded, arrested, and taken to San Jose where he was tried and sentenced to be hanged. Before his execution, he explained to a newspaper reporter why he had turned to a life of banditry.

> My career grew out of the circumstances by which I was surrounded. As I grew to manhood I was in the habit of attending balls and parties given by the native Californians, into which the Americans, then beginning to become numerous, would force themselves and shove the native-born men aside, monopolizing the dance and women. This was about 1852. A spirit of hatred and revenge took possession of me. I had numerous fights in defense of my countrymen. The officers were continually in pursuit of me. I believed we were unjustly and wrongfully deprived of the social rights that belonged to us.[5]

Both Vásquez and Murieta and many less famous California Mexican bandits of the nineteenth century must be viewed as products of the socioeconomic and political changes occurring in California after the gold rush. Though only a small minority of Mexicans resorted to armed resistance, their resentment of the Americanization of their society was shared by many Spanish-speaking Californians. Northern California society was transformed with such speed that Mexican people had little time to respond in any systematic way to this "second conquest." The same was not true of their cousins in the south. Mexican society remained intact over a decade longer because few Anglo Americans came south until the 1860's.

The Decline of Mexican Southern California

THOUGH THE GOLD RUSH attracted hundreds of Americans who settled in southern California pueblos, Anglos generally remained a minority in the "cow counties" (from San Luis Obispo to San Diego) during the 1850s. However, when Anglo Americans reached population parity with Mexicans in the early 1860s (see Table 1), they acquired political and economic control of the region. Much as in the north, Americans and Mexicans in the south during the 1850s and into the 1860s, with

Table 1: Total Mexican Population and Percentage of Population
in Selected California Cities, 1846–1890

City and Year	Total Population	Mexican Population	Percentage of Mexicans of Total Population
Los Angeles (city)[a]			
1846[b]	1,250	1,200	96.0%
1860	4,385	2,069	47.1
1870	5,728	2,160	37.7
1880	11,183	2,166	19.3
1890	50,395	NA[c]	—
Santa Barbara (town/city)[d]			
1846	—	1,000	—
1860	2,351	1,554	66.0%
1870	2,640	1,512	57.3
1880	3,460	932	26.9
1890	5,864	NA[c]	—
Santa Cruz (town)			
1846 (Monterey)	—	750	—
1860	1,812	388	21.4%
1870	1,920	134	7.0
1880	2,888	297	10.3
1890	—	NA[c]	—
San Jose (township)			
1846	—	700	—
1860	4,579	906	19.8%
1870	12,509	1,190	9.5
1880	18,156	1,114	6.1
1890	—	NA[c]	—

Sources: U.S. census population reports (1860–1890) and manuscript census schedules (1860–1880).

[a] Griswold del Castillo, The Los Angeles Barrio, 1850–1890, population figures for 1860–1880, p. 35.

[b] Approximate figures for 1846 cited in Weber, The Mexican Frontier, pp. 228–229. An estimated fifty foreigners resided in the pueblo of Los Angeles in 1846. Only fifty-three foreigners were enumerated in the 1844 Mexican census for the entire district of Los Angeles which included settlements outside the pueblo.

[c] The 1890 census manuscript schedules were destroyed by fire, so that population figures for Spanish-surnamed persons are not available.

[d] Camarillo, Chicanos in a Changing Society, pp. 116–117.

some exceptions, viewed one another with anger and resentment. To the Mexicans, "foreigners" were creating a new society which held little respect for the earlier residents and their traditions. To the Americans, "backward Mexicans" were impeding progress and Americanization.

The earliest and most visible form of conflict between Mexicans and Anglos of southern California was race-related. Particularly in the two main centers of population, Los Angeles and Santa Barbara, racial tension and violence erupted repeatedly, prompting historians to refer to the disorder of the 1850s as "race wars." Hangings by Anglo vigilantes and kangaroo courts which summarily sentenced Mexican defendants inflamed and frustrated the local Spanish-speaking population. This frustration often resulted in more violence, reflected in the many unsolved murders of both Anglos and Mexicans. Mexican banditry and quasi-revolutionary activity—such as the depredations of the Solomón Pico and Juan Flores gangs—then brought additional retaliation by Anglo lawmen and vigilantes. At first the rancheros and their families supported the Anglo laws and lawmen until they realized that Mexicans of all classes were being unjustly treated under the new system.[6]

Accompanying and helping to precipitate the violence were the attitudes of the newcomers toward Mexicans. Charles E. Huse, a transplanted easterner in Santa Barbara, described the Mexicans there as the "dregs of society. . . . The greatest part of the population is lazy, does not work, does not pay its debts, does not keep its word, is full of envy, of ill will, of cunning, craft and fraud, falsehood and ignorance." In the words of one vigilante, "To shoot these Greasers ain't the best way. . . . Give 'em a fair trial, and rope 'em up with all the majesty of the law. That's the cure." Reacting to such abuse during the 1850s, the editor of the Spanish-language newspaper in Los Angeles, *El Clamor Público,* lamented, "Mexicans alone have been the victims of the people's insane fury! Mexicans alone have been sacrificed on the gibbet and launched into eternity!" "California is lost to all Spanish Americans," Francisco Ramírez concluded in 1856. "This is the liberty and equality of our adopted land!"[7]

Widespread racial violence subsided by the early 1860s as Mexicans limited their contact with Anglos and as the criminal justice system meted out stiff prison sentences for those who violated "American law and order." Hostility now increasingly expressed itself in other forms, especially in competition for political power. In some locales, such as in the small pueblo of San Diego, community leaders accommodated to the political takeover by Anglos as a way to protect their own interests. In other pueblos, like Santa Barbara and San Salvador (in San Bernardino County), political campaigns and elections split along ethnic lines. Mexicans often voted as a bloc in efforts to defeat those Anglos identified as "anti-Mexican." In Los Angeles the Mexican electorate was less solidly aligned than in Santa Barbara and, as a result, lost the reins of political power as early as the 1860s. To consolidate their gains, the newcomers there established a system of balloting that clustered voters by blocks or neighborhoods. The resulting gerrymandered districts sliced up Mexican neighborhoods and reduced the possibility of an ethnic bloc vote. Some well-known ranchero families acquiesced in the political takeover by Anglos and were rewarded with political offices as late as the 1880s. Despite their Spanish surnames, they did not represent the Mexican minority. "Although superficially the Spanish-speaking did not appear to lack political representation," observes historian Richard Griswold del Castillo, "in fact they did. . . . For practical purposes the mass of laborers in the barrio remained politically inarticulate and unrepresented," and "not surprisingly, there is no evidence of any effort on their part [the Spanish-speaking elected officials] to ameliorate the pressing social and economic ills that plagued the barrio."[8]

By 1880 the gerrymandered Mexican community in Los Angeles had its counterpart in Santa Barbara. Mexican political influence was dealt a death blow when the last two remaining political spokesmen for the Spanish-speaking people — Councilman Caesar Lataillade and Sheriff Nicolás C. Covarrubias — either withdrew voluntarily or resigned under duress.[9]

Losses on the local level were followed by setbacks within the political parties themselves. The status of California Mexicans in party politics during the remainder of the nineteenth century was clearly illustrated in 1882 when, according to a delegate to the state Democratic convention, they were "deliberately kicked out of the party" and "treated with utter contempt."[10] Mexicans in the south had now joined their northern cousins in their exclusion from meaningful participation in the new political system.

The decline of political influence went hand in hand with economic loss. The rancho cattle industry boomed during the late 1840s and early 1850s due to the influx of the gold-rush population only to slump in the late 1850s. The importation of superior beef cattle from outside the state and the overgrazing of the range glutted the market. In the 1860s California cattle could be bought for almost nothing. This setback, together with increasing legal fees to validate land claims, took its toll. Though the process of land loss was slower in the south, rancheros in both sections eventually shared a common fate.

To survive during the slump in the cattle market and to pay attorneys' fees, rancheros deeded away large tracts of land. Unscrupulous lawyers worsened the situation. A common practice was for lawyers to persuade unsuspecting Mexican landowners to entrust them with the power of attorney on all matters. Dozens of rancheros — such as the Domínguez family of Santa Barbara County, who lost 75,000 acres — relinquished vast holdings because they naïvely placed too much confidence in certain Anglo attorneys. Parker H. French, a state legislator from San Luis Obispo, for example, gained the trust of local rancheros and used forged power-of-attorney documents to mortgage or sell "every ranch in the county worth the trouble."[11]

The legal problems of many rancheros seemed minor beside those created by the winter floods of 1862 which killed thousands of cattle. Following the floods was a three-year drought that proved even more disastrous. The combination of flood and drought decimated the pastoral economy. Rancheros sought to ward off total economic collapse by borrowing cash at usurious interest rates, a practice begun in the 1850s. They succeeded only in "borrowing" themselves out of their land grants when the loans came due. The fate of Mexican farmers and ranchers in San Diego was typical. In 1860 they comprised over thirty percent of all employed males, but by 1880 they accounted for less than two percent. Their counterparts in Santa Barbara suffered a similar decline, from over twenty-four percent to seven percent during the same period. "This was the beginning of poverty for many old California families," remarked Dario

Oreña, a once wealthy Santa Barbara ranchero whose land-holdings were mortgaged and then lost to Anglo merchants.[12] Many ranches were also sold at public auction for delinquent tax payments. By 1880 the land tenure system in southern California had been as radically altered as that in the north. Anglos now owned most of the former Mexican land grants, nearly all of which were soon subdivided and sold to other Americans.[13]

The wholesale breakup of the ranchos and the end of the cattle industry in California had serious consequences for both Mexicans and Americans. Rancho life, of course, was a thing of the past. For those who lived in the towns, loss of traditional pueblo communal lands — usually sold by local city councils once they were controlled by Anglos — meant that subsistence farming and grazing were no longer possible. As the local and regional pastoral economy eroded, most skilled and semiskilled wage earners such as leather craftsmen, vaqueros, and a host of other workers associated with the seasonal roundups and slaughters became jobless. Economic depression, unemployment, and increasing poverty were now the lot of most Mexican people.

For Americans, on the other hand, the dismemberment of the Mexican land-ownership system paved the way for the introduction of a new economic order based on agricultural development in the hinterlands and commercial expansion in the towns. The coming of the railroad in 1869 contributed greatly to Anglo success, but so, too, did the attainment of political and economic power. Americans could develop their institutions and economic interests without exerting much energy to dislodge the Mexicans. Fueled by the migration of nearly a million new residents from other parts of the U.S. during the last three decades of the century, the population of the state soared from 620,000 in 1870 to nearly a million and a half by 1900.[14]

Barrioization, Adaptation, and Occupational Change

L AND LOSS AND political disenfranchisement during the two decades after the Mexican War forged a new reality for Mexican people in California. Residential segregation and a new working-class status came to characterize their lives. Barrioization — the formation of Mexican neighborhoods socially, culturally, and politically segregated from Anglo sections of cities and towns — and shifts in occupations were the two principal changes during the last quarter of the century. Though these developments differed somewhat between north and south, between rural and urban areas, they were the products of a process begun in the 1850s. Barrioization and the entrance of Mexicans into the expanding labor market occurred rapidly after Americans acquired the land and achieved political hegemony.

The old Mexican pueblos were viewed by most Americans as "foreign," "backward," and undesirable locations in which to live. Thus, Mexicans were de facto segregated in their communities as Anglo sections of the towns and cities developed. In the north, the process of barrioization was much more swift, occurring during the 1850s in most places. The small San Francisco Mexican population near the mission was overwhelmed by 1850, though the Spanish-speaking people continued to occupy this district of the growing metropolis. Down the coast from San Francisco, the small Mexican populations in Santa Cruz (known earlier as Branciforte) and Monterey soon became minority communities in the wake of the gold rush. Santa Cruz Mexicans, for example, fell from majority to minority status between 1845 and 1850 (from fifty-six percent to twenty-seven percent of the population); by 1880 they numbered only 297, slightly more than their total in 1845 and a mere ten percent of the city's population. In San Jose the number of Mexicans increased in the early 1850s with the arrival of Sonoran miners expelled from the gold fields. From approximately 700 in 1846 the Spanish-surnamed population in the township grew to nearly 1,200 in 1870. Further increases in the area's Spanish-speaking population occurred during the 1870s when the New Almaden mercury mines, located about thirteen miles south of

San Jose, required a sizable work force. Mexican miners lived on the grounds of the Quicksilver Mining company in what became known as "Mexican Town," an area distinct from "English Town" inhabited by skilled Cornish immigrant miners. "It was mutually understood and for a great many years strictly adhered to," noted a mine superintendent in the 1920s, "that Mexicans and their families would not be permitted to take their residence within the sacred precincts of the English camp." An infirmary separate from that used by the English miners — established "on account of national prejudices," according to a mining inspector in 1885 — and a separate school and church were built in Mexican Town, making it a self-contained community. During most of the late nineteenth century, as many as a thousand Mexican miners and their relatives lived in the houses clustered on the hill amidst the numerous mine shafts. [15]

In the southern part of the state, barrioization did not occur until the 1870s when tens of thousands of Americans from throughout the U.S. converged on southern California in response to the tourist-real estate booms of 1873–1875 and especially 1887–1888. New railroad and stage connections, together with new accommodations for visitors, prompted promoters to invest heavily in the development of southern California. The population influx quickly submerged the Mexican population. Only a small number of the once wealthy Spanish-speaking elite escaped the subsequent social and geographic segregation and were effectively assimilated into American society, largely through intermarriage. [16]

To the great majority of Mexican residents in the emerging barrios, the sections of cities outside their neighborhoods were unfriendly at best and hostile at worst. Though the barrios resulted partly from the efforts of entrepreneurial Anglos to develop the "American" sections of the cities, their emergence also reflected the desire of Mexicans to create a haven for traditional customs characteristic of the old pueblos. In the Sonora Town barrio of Los Angeles, the historic pueblo area of Santa Barbara, and Old Town San Diego, Mexicans maintained much of their former life style in the face of increasing social and residential segregation practiced by Anglos.

Thus, barrioization ensured the persistence of Mexican society in California. During a period of tremendous change outside

the pueblos-turned-barrios, the segregation of Mexican residents in their communities reinforced the use of the Spanish
language, religious practices, cultural and social activities, and
family ties. Most Mexicans seldom interacted with Anglos and
spent little time, aside from working hours, away from the
confines of their barrios. Though certain social practices of the
pre-American period vanished — such as the large Mexican wed-
dings, horse races, and bull-bear fights — others persisted, such
as cockfights, barbecues, fandangos, and horsemanship con-
tests. Some recreational activities — cockfights, for example —
were considered barbarous by Anglos, and although outlawed
by local authorities, they were commonplace in the barrios.
Barrioization also fostered maintenance of close family ties during a time when poverty and seasonal job migrations strained
relationships. Families relied more on one another during the
hard times, and extended families of grandparents, their children, and other relatives maintained ties between the younger
and older generations. Moreover, Catholic religious traditions,
practiced at home and in church and consisting of prayers and
festivities in the name of patron saints and the holy family,
cushioned the hard realities of life for most Mexican families.
The celebrations in honor of the many patron saints' days
also provided opportunities for frequent social gatherings in a
chapel, a plaza courtyard, or a neighbor's back yard. Some of
these practices, in particular the extended family and neighborhood barbecues, persisted into the twentieth century. "When I
was a kid — 1911, 1912, 1913 — all the Spanish families would
gather in Santa Monica Canyon for a barbecue," recalled Joaquín de la Peña, a descendant of a ranchero family in Los
Angeles. "We'd kill a couple of steers . . . , two or three barrels
of beer . . . and have a three-day celebration." "Life in those
days was different. . . . Everybody knew everybody," he remi-
nisced, and "the Anglos stayed away from us. . . . We all spoke
Spanish."[17]

Barrioization also prompted Mexicans throughout the state
to devise ways for coping with their minority status. Besides
preserving much of their earlier culture, they created new social,
political, and cultural organizations. Some served to maintain a
Mexican nationalism by sponsoring patriotic and cultural celebrations in commemoration of important holidays such as Mexi-

can Independence Day. La Junta Patriótica de Juárez (Juárez Patriotic Group or Club) in Los Angeles and La Junta Patriótica Mexicana in Santa Barbara, for example, staged gala celebrations for predominantly Mexican audiences beginning in the 1860s. Other clubs were primarily political associations, such as San Francisco's Spanish American Independent Political Club, which supported the nomination of Spanish-speaking candidates for election to public offices. Other organizations focused on mutual-aid benefits for their members. In Los Angeles, for example, La Sociedad Hispano-Americana de Benéfica Mutua provided life insurance, loans, and medical insurance in addition to other social services. Besides the formally organized groups, there were a host of ephemeral organizations that sponsored Sunday dances and barbecues, traveling troupes of acrobats, musical and theatrical groups, and other events.[18]

Perhaps the most obvious expressions of a changing culture and consciousness within Mexican American society in California are found in the many newspapers published in the second half of the century. More than two dozen Spanish-language newspapers appeared in California between 1870 and 1910. Besides providing news about events in Mexico and thereby maintaining a link to the mother country, they also printed information about local cultural, literary, and social activities. The newspapers were also central to the psychological well-being of their readership. They expressed pride in Mexican American ethnicity, presented minority viewpoints, and denounced the discrimination and racism faced daily by Spanish-speaking citizens. "The Mexican-American community was convinced," notes a historian of these newspapers, "that one source of this oppression was the racism which the Anglo-Americans brought with them from the eastern and southern states." As a result, "editorial policy often included a pledge to fight for the dignity of all Hispano-Americans in the face of Anglo-American prejudice . . . often fostered by the American press which they [the Spanish-language newspapers] brought under severe criticism for prolonging racial strife and misunderstanding in California."[19] Though a majority of Mexicans could not read, those who did passed on information by word of mouth.

Ethnic consciousness as expressed in the newspapers and organizations contributed greatly to the persistence of Mexican society. This was important since racial hostility was only one of the threats faced by communities. Out-migration, economic stagnation, and physical deterioration of dwellings were serious enough to destroy the vitality of the smaller Mexican communities. Long-forgotten San Salvador (also known as Aqua Mansa) in the San Bernardino Valley and Old Town San Diego by the early 1900s were among the casualties. In little more than two generations, Mexican families had moved from the decaying buildings of San Salvador and Old Town. Such abandonment was due in large part to the search for employment in the growing "American" towns nearby. Mexicans in the larger communities of Los Angeles, Santa Barbara, and San Jose escaped this problem since they could find work outside the barrio and then return to their families and neighborhoods in the evening.

Much like the process of barrioization, the incorporation of Mexicans into the new labor market in the cities and hinterlands was well under way by the last two decades of the nineteenth century. Land loss and the decline of the pastoral economy meant that fewer Mexicans could work in the cattle trade and in related jobs. In addition, the rise of an agricultural economy in the rural areas and an urban economy geared to construction and to the service trades meant that American farmers and capitalists needed a large labor force, preferably a cheap one, in order to ensure high profits. During the first quarter-century after the Mexican War, Indians and Chinese supplied a good part of these labor needs. However, by the 1870s the increased demand for unskilled and semiskilled labor (such as farm workers, cannery workers, day laborers, and teamsters) could not be met by the declining Indian population nor by the Chinese, the latter of whom were being systematically excluded from most localities and sought refuge in San Francisco's Chinatown. Into this vacuum came the Mexican workers no longer able to eke out a living doing part-time work in the dying cattle trade. They entered the labor market both as individuals and family units in order to survive. In southern California women often were the first members of the community to acquire new types of employment as they found jobs in the fruit canneries and as seasonal farm workers. They also worked as domestic servants, hotel maids, and laundresses, and often became street vendors selling homemade tamales and other foods. Men worked in construction-related jobs as ditch diggers, street graders, and draymen. Some were miners, such as those in the New Almaden mercury mines of San Jose, while others worked as gardeners, servants, and railroad section-gang hands. Men also worked as seasonal migrant farm laborers. For many, the Chicano working-class experience involved the employment of the entire family as a unit. Husbands and wives were joined by their children during seasonal harvests because the income from the work of all able-bodied family members was essential to making a living.[20]

The transition for Mexican males from pastoral-related work to the menial labor associated with the new economy must have been difficult to accept. Likewise, the responsibilities of Mexican females now employed outside the home for the first time must have created new tensions that accompanied their changing roles. Yet economic necessity forced all who could — including children as young as seven or eight years old — to work. The impact of these new occupational experiences and responsibilities on the Chicano family and, by extension, on the community must have been profound, though it is difficult to determine because of the lack of available evidence.

In the 1890s the employment pattern for Mexicans had stabilized. Between sixty and ninety percent occupied the lowest rung of the occupational ladder and were confined to menial, unskilled jobs. They lived precariously close to abject poverty and bare subsistence. Few entered the skilled trades and even fewer found white-collar jobs of any kind. An observation made around the turn of the century by a Spanish-speaking clergyman in San Bernardino captured vividly the condition of most Chicanos. "The passing years have wrought many changes to the people and to the state," declared Father Juan Caballería. "Most of the old settlers have passed away. . . . Their descendants are scattered, some of them having fallen on evil days" as "victims of distressing poverty; but many of them, in spite of the disadvantages under which they labor, still maintain the traditional virtues of their fathers."[21]

As California Mexicans entered the twentieth century, they had few successes about which they could rejoice. In two generations they had lost their lands and political influence; they had been socially and geographically isolated in their pueblos-turned-barrios; they had been displaced from traditional, pastoral-related occupations and forced ofttimes into demeaning employment. Their society in less than forty years had been forever altered. Yet they had also retained their distinctiveness as an ethnic minority and had weathered the turbulent times of overt racial violence which conceivably could have destroyed their communities. They had clung tenaciously to customs, language, and religion. Hardship seemed to confirm them in their determination to survive; their religious celebrations were community affairs; their social halls resounded with laughter, folk music, and song; and their cultural pageantry was joyful and rich.

This new Mexican American reality carried over into the next century and helped shape the experiences of future generations of Chicanos.

CHAPTER THREE

The Emergence of Contemporary Chicano Society: 1900–1930

THE DEVELOPMENTS OF the early twentieth century set the character of contemporary California society. During the three decades after 1900 the state matured and moved swiftly into national prominence in the wake of dramatic population growth and advances in agriculture, transportation, petroleum, motion pictures, and tourism. Urbanization and industrialization also highlighted this era. California's Mexican population reflected — and sometimes reeled from — these larger developments. An influx of migrants from Mexico and rapid expansion in agricultural and urban demands for labor meant changes for Chicano society, but the changes were accompanied by continuing and deepening socioeconomic cleavages and racial conflict. By the eve of the Great Depression, California had proven to be a "land of golden opportunity" for many people, but not for the majority of Chicanos who remained basically in the same position that they occupied at the turn of the century.

North from Mexico

THE YEAR 1900, often used to symbolize entry into a new era, had special meaning for Chicano people. The older Mexican pueblo society and barrios were still visible, but other developments were obscuring their identity. New Mexican neighborhoods now began to dot the rural and urban landscape as the Mexican population increased substantially during the next thirty years. Conceivably, the changes that swept the state during the early 1900s could have submerged completely the Mexican presence had it not been for the huge immigration from Mexico.

California's modern economy rested on the labor of working-class people of whom Mexican men and women formed a large part. As early as the 1890s Mexicans were recruited by U.S. railroads interested in cheap, unskilled labor. These workers were joined by others who merely walked or waded across an open border. Prior to the 1920s, Mexicans came and went with little difficulty. Railway lines into central Mexico, completed before 1900 with the help of U.S. corporate financing, made travel to the north inexpensive and efficient. The number of immigrants who came to the U.S. prior to 1900 is difficult to determine since official statistics were almost non-existent at the time. Though probably less than ten thousand for the decade of the 1890s, these migrants represented the trickle that became the tidal wave of the 1900s.

The forces that spawned large-scale Mexican immigration intensified during the early twentieth century. The expansion in Mexico of the hacienda system — feudal-like farms and ranches characterized by extensive land holdings — squeezed out rural peasants at the same time that inflation eroded the meager wages paid to workers. Political discontent and repression during the regime of dictator Porfirio Díaz led thousands to flee their homeland. North of the border, in the American Southwest and California in particular, there was unprecedented growth in agriculture, railroad development, and mining, as well as rapid expansion of the construction, service, and manufacturing industries in the urban centers. Mexicans were attracted to or recruited for these industries as unskilled and semiskilled workers.

The Mexican Revolution of 1910, which first expelled Díaz and then produced fighting among various factions until the 1920s, unleashed a tremendous migration from Mexico. "In my youth I worked as a house servant," Pablo Mares recounted, "but as I grew older I wanted to be independent." "I was able through great efforts to start a little store in my town, Guadalajara, . . . but I had to come to the United States, because it was impossible to live down there with so many revolutions." Political instability, economic chaos, bloody civil war, and terrible poverty forced hundreds of thousands of Mexicans such as Mares to flee northward. Between 1910 and 1930 nearly a tenth of the entire population of Mexico fled to the U.S. Accurate figures are unavailable, but certainly more than a million persons (685,000 legal immigrants and probably an equal number without documents) crossed from Mexico. Though most entered through Texas, and the majority remained there, tens of thousands headed for Arizona and California. In 1915 Mares, like so many others, went first to Ciudad Juárez and then to El Paso. "There I put myself under contract to go to work on the tracks," he recalled, and that labor soon brought him west to California. "I was for a while in Los Angeles working in cement work, which is very hard," Mares remembered as he traced his migratory path across Kansas, Oklahoma, Texas, and Arizona in search of employment. Following the rails, he and others like him, often including entire families, found work in the seasonal agricultural harvests of California or as unskilled laborers in the cities.[1]

Most immigrants came from Mexico's northern and south-central states of Michoacán, Jalisco, Zacatecas, Durango, Chihuahua, and Sonora. Though Texas remained for decades the principal destination (fifty-six percent of the total immigrant population in 1910 and forty-two percent in 1930), the popularity of California increased significantly (from fifteen percent to thirty-one percent of the total immigrant population during the same period). This trend of preferred migration to California — reflecting economic opportunties, both real and imagined — increased with every decade.[2]

Table 2 : Total Mexican Population and Percentage of Population
in Selected California Cities, 1900–1930

City and Year	Total Population	Mexican Population (low-high range)	Percentage of Mexicans of Total City Population (low-high range)
Los Angeles			
1900	102,479	3,000–5,000	2.9– 4.9%
1910	319,198	9,678–29,738	3.0– 9.3
1920	576,673	29,757–50,000	5.2– 8.7
1930	1,238,048	97,116–190,000	7.8–15.3
San Diego			
1900	17,700	638–893	3.6– 5.0%
1910	39,578	1,588–1,595	4.0– 4.0
1920	74,683	3,563–4,028	4.7– 5.4
1930	147,995	9,266–20,000	6.3–13.5
Santa Barbara			
1900	6,587	1,108–1,551	16.8–23.5%
1910	11,659	1,644–2,221	14.1–19.0
1920	19,441	2,558–2,888	13.1–14.8
1930	33,613	3,279–5,157	9.7–15.3

Source: Camarillo, *Chicanos in a Changing Society,* pp. 200–201.

Those refugees arriving in the U.S. prior to World War I
were more diversified in their backgrounds than those coming
later. The majority were rural workers, but they were joined by
professional people, urban craftsmen, and ousted officeholders
fleeing the revolution. Economic hardships and unemployment
in Mexico also drove merchants and white-collar workers to the
U.S. Most of these immigrants found that job opportunities,
regardless of prior skills learned in Mexico, were usually re-
stricted to unskilled and semiskilled manual labor.[3]

The thousands who arrived in California prior to the First
World War were followed by even larger numbers during the
postwar decade. These later immigrants came primarily from
the working class and included nuclear and extended families,
women alone with children, single men, and single women.
They came from cities as well as from the countryside. In the
burgeoning agricultural economy of the state, they quickly
became the chief source of seasonal farm labor and contributed
to the spectacular growth of the state's agribusiness. In the

Imperial Valley, for example, Mexicans in 1918 were the largest pool of agricultural laborers and formed by 1927 over a third (approximately twenty thousand persons) of the total population in the area. "Large-scale production would be impossible without the Mexican field labor," a valley produce company executive remarked in 1927. "Without the Mexicans," he added, "costs would be increased fifty percent." As corporate agriculture expanded in California, labor-intensive farm production became even more dependent on Mexicans. By the late 1920s, Mexican workers accounted for eighty percent of the farm workers in southern California and were the preferred laborers on the vast majority of large farms throughout the state. In the cities as well, particularly those in southern California, Mexicans constituted a large part of the growing working class. In the transportation industry they provided between seventy and ninety percent of the railroad section hands in California and the Southwest, and though not as heavily concentrated in other areas of the state's economy, large percentages of Mexicans in California were employed in low blue-collar jobs in the construction, canning and packing, garment, and service industries. Much of the economic activity in agriculture and related industries was thus dependent on the labor of Mexican workers.[4]

Patterns of Residence

M EXICAN IMMIGRANTS TO CALIFORNIA often lived and worked next to those residents descended from colonists of the late 1700s and early 1800s. By the early 1900s, however, the foreign-born Mexicans far exceeded in numbers the native-born Mexican Californians. The newcomers frequently followed patterns established by the previous generation of nineteenth-century Mexicans, but they also initiated new patterns of work and residence. Mexicans typically lived close to their employment in industry, manufacturing, commerce, transportation, and agriculture. In older urban areas such as Los Angeles, Mexicans naturally migrated to neighborhoods where a Mexican community already existed, but as their numbers increased they moved east beyond the central plaza area and across the river, settling among European immigrants in Lincoln Heights, Boyle Heights, the Brooklyn Avenue district, and Belvedere. The origins of today's population of over 600,000 Chicano residents in east Los Angeles dates from migrations of the early twentieth century. In addition to the rapidly growing Mexican population in the eastside, enclaves of Mexicans formed throughout the greater Los Angeles area in such locales as Long Beach, Compton, Watts, Santa Monica, Venice, and Wilmington. Elsewhere in coastal California, certain sections where Mexicans had not lived previously became sizable barrios by 1930 — such as Logan Heights in San Diego and the lower eastside of Santa Barbara. In the agricultural valleys, such as San Joaquin and Imperial, new rural Mexican *colonias* (colonies) formed as seasonal workers became permanently settled. In the Imperial Valley, for example, the small communities of Brawley, El Centro, Calexico, and Westmoreland had "Mexican sections" usually located across the railroad tracks from the Anglo neighborhoods. In Sacramento, Mexicans located in the "lower quarter" below Fifth Street amid Asian and European immigrants. "For the Mexicans the barrio was a colony of refugees," recalled Ernesto Galarza, a future labor and community organizer and scholar, who with his mother and two uncles arrived in the state capital during the early 1910s from a small mountain village in western Mexico.

> In the years between our arrival and the First World War, the colonia grew and spilled out from the lower part of town. Some families moved into the alley shacks east of the Southern Pacific tracks, close to the canneries and warehouses and across the river among the orchards and rice mills. . . . The colonia was like a sponge that was beginning to leak along the edges, squeezed between the levee, the railroad tracks, and the river front. But it wasn't squeezed dry, because it kept filling with newcomers who found families who took in boarders: basements, alleys, shanties, rundown rooming houses and flop joints where they could live. . . . Crowded as it was, the colonia found a place for these "chicanos," the name by which we called an unskilled worker born in Mexico and just arrived in the United States.[5]

Up and down the state during the first thirty years of the century, Mexican urban barrios and rural colonias, some old and some new, characterized a pattern of residence that still predominates. Though each Mexican community possessed unique qualities that differentiated it from others, the common denominators of Mexican neighborhoods, regardless of locality and size, were segregation and poverty.[6]

The barrioization process continued to include the proliferation of community organizations and the reinforcement of Mexican culture and society. Just as Mexicans during the second half of the nineteenth century had created new ethnic and nationalistic organizations that helped maintain the cohesiveness of their communities, later immigrants also contributed to the building of strong community organizations. Mutual aid societies were organized virtually everywhere Mexicans settled. Many joined already established *mutualistas,* while others created new ones to meet vital community needs. They provided sick and death benefits; social, patriotic, and cultural activities; protection of civil rights; and aid in adjusting to life in America. Networks of these organizations created linkages among Mexican communities and some served as labor organizations. In 1927, for example, a group of Mexican mutual aid societies from the rural valley towns and urban metropolitan areas in southern California combined to form the first umbrella labor union of Mexican workers, La Confederación de Uniones Obreras Mexicanas or CUOM (see Chapter 4).

Women were instrumental in these organization-building activities, sometimes participating jointly with men and other times establishing auxiliaries of their own. Women founded the Unión Femenil Mexicana, for example, as a parallel group to La Unión Patriótica Benéfica Mexicana Independiente, an organization with local chapters in many southern California barrios which sponsored social, patriotic, and mutual aid activities. In some cases women headed local theatrical and musical groups, such as Club La Rosita in Santa Barbara, and organized chapters of the Cruz Azul Mexicana, the Mexican equivalent of the American Red Cross. Women were enthusiastic promoters of social events such as dances, barbecues, fiestas, and picnics as well as community self-help and welfare activities that were crucial to the well-being of barrio residents.

Commmunity organizations built on and reinforced the existing culture and heritage that Mexicans had established in

California. But the waves of immigrants added new features to Mexican society, particularly by maintaining strong identification with Mexico and by strengthening the role of the Catholic Church in Chicano communities. Everywhere Mexicans settled, whether in new barrios or in the old pueblo areas, they supported the establishment of local parishes, often named after the Virgin of Guadalupe, the beloved Virgin Mary who, according to pious legend, appeared in Mexico in 1531 and subsequently became the revered patroness of Mexican people. New church-sponsored activities included *jamaicas* or fund-raising and social bazaars and the Guadalupana groups, which sponsored a host of religious and social events under parish auspices. Both church and community groups promoted an identification with Mexico by organizing patriotic celebrations and by maintaining continuity of cultural, linguistic, social, and religious activities that regularly brought Mexicans together. Fiestas, patriotic festivities, and an array of relegous ceremonies (baptisms, first communions, confirmations, and other traditional rites) took place within virtually all neighborhoods and contributed to a vibrant cultural and social milieu for Mexican people. These neighborhoods in turn fostered the growth of Spanish-language movie and vaudeville theaters and bookstores, Mexican restaurants and shops, all of which created a distinctive Mexican American ambiance.[7]

As in earlier decades, this unique environment was fostered by forces internal to Mexican communities, such as the desire to live close to one another, as well as by external forces which Mexicans did not control — the de facto segregation maintained by racially restrictive real-estate covenants and discriminatory hiring practices. Thus, barrioization in the early part of the century reflected positive elements (cultural, ethnic, and linguistic reinforcement) as well as negative forces (impoverishment, physical deterioration of neighborhoods, and lack of adequate municipal services).

Patterns of Work

R ESIDENTIAL PATTERNS revealed patterns of employment since Mexicans generally lived near their work. In San Bernardino, Santa Barbara, San Jose, and San Diego they concentrated near the canneries or the railroad freight yards. In Los Angeles they first lived in the downtown plaza area near the railroad maintenance yards· and new construction· sites. As manufacturing concerns migrated further east and south from the downtown area, workers moved in those directions. Likewise, the rural towns, such as El Centro, Fresno, and Salinas, attracted Mexican farmworkers, both permanent and seasonal residents.

About 1915 Gonzalo Galván came under contract to California as a railroad section hand, as did thousands of other immigrants. When he reached the railroad camp, he later recalled, "There were a number of Mexicans at the station who turned out to be from the same town that we were from, and they told us not to go out and work on the tracks because they paid little and would mistreat us"—a warning that proved accurate when the foreman refused to provide Galván and his friend with provisions until they each had worked for three days. In another case, Carlos Almanzán came to Los Angeles from Michoacán via El Paso and began working as a laborer while living on the Simon Brick Company grounds. He received four dollars for eight hours work, "but what eight hours!" he exclaimed. "I was left almost dead, especially the first days." Almanzán organized a back-to-Mexico effort among the Mexicans who lived on the brick company grounds and declared before his departure, "I don't believe that I will ever return to this country for I have spent the hardest days of my life; it is here where I have worked the hardest and earned the least. . . . Besides the people here don't like us, for even the Japanese treat Mexicans without considerations of any kind." The experiences of Galván and Almanzán were common among the tens of thousands of Mexican immigrants who came to California before the Depression, and who continued to come north regardless of the treatment.[8]

The size of the laboring class expanded during the early

twentieth century at the same time that the types of jobs available to Mexicans increased. Such traditional jobs as hod carriers, railroad/railway section-gang members, and construction day laborers continued to be filled by Mexicans. In addition, newer jobs in the factories, slaughterhouses, garment industry, food processing plants, and other burgeoning industries attracted Chicano workers, but these jobs did not necessarily translate into improved occupational status as measured by higher wages or better working conditions.

The number of Mexican women working in the urban areas also increased in response to the demands of new industries, particularly the garment factories, and expansions in food processing and canning. In Los Angeles during the late 1920s, according to labor analyst Paul S. Taylor, "the largest numbers of Mexican women . . . were employed in packing houses and canneries of various kinds, followed by the clothing [industry], needle trades, and laundries." Most women were compelled to work in order to help keep their families afloat financially, particularly when a husband or sibling was unemployed or otherwise unable to work. Economic necessity forced daughters and mothers to accept mostly menial, unskilled jobs; a small minority, however, worked outside the home in order to earn extra money and to be independent. A Mexican woman working in Los Angeles and interviewed for Taylor's study in 1926–1927 typified the thousands of immigrant women who sought employment because of financial need:

> She first came to Los Angeles because her husband was not making enough to support their family of seven. Of the seventy-five dollars which she earned monthly, thirty dollars was spent for a three-room dwelling, which left only forty-five dollars for all other expenses.

Another young woman, according to Taylor's interviewer, "came to the United States in 1915 with her husband who worked in the Imperial Valley until 1925 when they moved to Los Angeles. . . . She started working when her husband temporarily lost his job, and she continued to work temporarily when they were in need of money." Some women secured skilled and semi-skilled employment as machine operators and a few were well-trained stenographers or bookkeepers, but these were exceptions.

Though Los Angeles provided the largest labor market for women, Mexican girls and women in communities from San Diego to San Jose labored as cannery workers, laundresses, hotel maids, and farm workers, and in other jobs on either a full-time or part-time basis.[9]

Though Mexicans found employment in the expanding work force in California, their jobs did not provide much upward occupational mobility. Many employers were biased about the ability of Mexican workers to perform anything but manual labor, and they often revealed this prejudice by paying Mexicans less than Anglos for the same work. The wage differentials, dead-end jobs, and a general lack of skilled trade experience resulted in few good occupational opportunities. Social and occupational mobility studies for the period universally conclude that upward occupational mobility for Mexican workers was rare even for the first- and second-generation native-born. These conditions sparked labor conflict between Mexican workers and their employers in both the cities and rural areas.

Rural and Urban Labor Conflict

THE FIRST RECORDED STRIKE in California agriculture involved Mexican workers. In 1903 the Japanese-Mexican Labor Union called a strike in Oxnard to protest the exploitative labor contract system, to obtain recognition of the union, and to achieve better working conditions in general for its sugar-beet workers. This strike initiated the farm worker-grower disputes that still characterize California agribusiness. Though the union achieved its demands, most labor organizations during the period failed to gain concessions from growers. Contributing to these failures were the major national labor unions. Prior to the 1930s, the American Federation of Labor avoided organizing unskilled workers of any nationality, especially migratory farm workers, on the grounds that they were "unorganizable." Though ignored by the AFL, Mexican and other farm workers did not go unnoticed. By 1910 the Industrial Workers of the World (IWW) had organized unskilled workers in the mining, lumber, and farm-labor camps in California.

The so-called Wobblies first attempted to organize agricultural workers living in deplorable conditions at the Durst hop ranch in Wheatland. Also causing resentment there were the below-subsistence wages and a company store which charged excessively for goods. Efforts by authorities to break up an IWW meeting resulted in the 1913 Wheatland Riot which brought about the death of the sheriff, the district attorney, and two workers. A manhunt for two IWW leaders culminated in a trial and sentences of life imprisonment for both. Authorities brutally suppressed all IWW efforts to organize workers. Though the IWW continued its activities after World War I, it could not succeed in an American society frightened by the "red scare" and suspicious of "bolshevik agitators." Farm workers remained without union help during most of the 1920s.

The 1928 cantaloupe strike by La Unión de Trabajadores del Valle Imperial (Union of Imperial Valley Workers) — an organization created by leaders of local mutual aid societies — foreshadowed the wave of agricultural strikes of the 1930s. Mexican workers organized to increase their wages and to eliminate the abuses of labor contractors. Growers refused to discuss the issues with the union and instead called upon the authorities to conduct mass arrests. The power of the growers and repressive tactics used by law enforcement agencies, such as deportation and intimidation of workers, broke the strike. Those Mexican workers who were not deported went back to their jobs. [10]

Labor conflict also occurred in the cities, though most of the strikes took place before 1910. In Los Angeles, the Pacific Electric Railway strike of 1903 involved primarily Mexican section-gang workers who staged a walkout for better working conditions and union recognition. Like most such activity of the period, arrests, deportations, and hiring of scabs broke the back of the strike. An exception occurred in the same year as the railway strike when Santa Barbara Mexicans went on strike against the local fruit cannery and achieved at least part of their pay demands. [11]

Most Mexican workers, however, did not engage in labor militancy. They avoided involvement because of fear and intimidation: fear of losing their jobs, fear of arrest and police brutality, and especially fear of deportation. After all, most Mexican workers were technically illegal immigrants, and their fear of deportation intensified during the 1920s when many Americans expressed alarm at the growth of the Mexican population.

The "Mexican Problem"

THE DECADE OF THE 1920s marked the height of immigration from Mexico. As the volume of that migration peaked, the visibility of Mexicans in the public eye also increased. In the cities, the barrios had grown tremendously, so much so that the Chicano neighborhoods in Los Angeles, San Diego, Riverside, and many other places were attracting the attention of public health, school, and welfare bureau officials. In rural areas, the "Mexican side of town" also became more obvious to everyone. Californians by the late 1920s began questioning the notion that Mexicans were a temporary population—that they would stay only long enough to earn money and then return to Mexico. Recognition of the Mexicans' desire to remain in the U.S. focused public attention on what was termed the "Mexican problem," a problem defined variously by different sectors of California society. Social workers and teachers looked upon the problem in terms of assimilation. Labor union officials wanted to prevent Mexicans from taking jobs away from Americans. Protestant clergy focused on the threat of popery from an increased Roman Catholic population while eugenicists feared possible miscegenation and dilution of Anglo American life and culture.

In response to these impressions of the "Mexican problem," pundits offered a variety of solutions. School leaders designed so-called Americanization programs that allegedly fostered assimilation and helped Mexicans become productive American citizens. The educational curriculum forced these students to learn English (those who spoke Spanish in the classroom or on the playground were often punished) and to instill in them American cultural values. Educators also introduced vocational programs which they believed would produce a corps of semi-skilled and skilled workers in the expanding industrial economy. Though the Americanization programs were partly successful in forcing changes in linguistic and cultural values in young Chicano pupils, these programs did not reckon with undesirable effects: cultural clashes between what was taught at school and what was learned at home, breeding of inferiority complexes, and beginning a legacy of school failure. As the number of Mexican children dramatically increased in California public schools during the 1920s, another characteristic of their education developed: segregation. In 1927, Mexican children — over seventy percent of whom had been born in the U.S. and thus were U.S. citizens — accounted for nearly ten percent of all students in state elementary schools; the great majority were concentrated in southern California counties (eighty-eight percent) with over fifty percent in Los Angeles County schools. This large increase in pupils typically resulted in ther separation from Anglo students. "One of the first demands made from a community in which there is a large Mexican population is for a separate school," a California educator observed in 1920. "The reasons advanced for this demand," she continued, "are generally from a selfish viewpoint of the English-speaking public and are based largely on the theory that the Mexican is a menace to the health and morals of the rest of the community." Though Mexicans were not legally segregated in schools as were other racial minority groups, they were, according to a historian of racial segregation in the state's public schools, "by far the most segregated group in California public education by the end of the 1920s." Because such formidable obstacles faced this generation of Chicano children, one should not be surprised that so few advanced into high school. For example, in one school district where Mexicans constituted thirty percent of the elementary school population, they accounted for only about four percent of those enrolled in the high schools. Even fewer graduated.[12]

   Though the public schools were not conduits to high school or college for Chicanos, they certainly served as Americanizing institutions which facilitated changes in language and behavior. Other public institutions, especially the social service agencies during the 1920s, also tried their hand at Americanizing Mexicans, some using such naïve tactics as teaching Mexican housewives how to cook "American food" and how to maintain proper "American households." In addition to public agencies and schools, other Americanization programs sought to convert

Mexican Catholics to Protestantism. The Methodists, Presbyterians, and Baptists were the most avid proselytizers among Mexicans. Though the Protestant churches and public institutions enjoyed some success in their respective conversion programs, Americanization of the Mexican people was a slow process which required decades in the face of determined efforts to cling to cultural practices brought from Mexico.[13]

Other solutions to the "Mexican problem" came from labor unions and xenophobes who clamored for immigration restrictions. Riding a wave of nativist sentiment, they first secured passage of the Immigration Act of 1924, which effectively cut off immigration from Europe and Asia, and then focused their attention on Mexico. Ethnocentric rhetoric, together with labor union claims that Mexicans displaced American workers, became standard fare on the floor of Congress between 1924 and 1928. Anti-restrictionists—most of whom were agribusinessmen and industrialists dependent on large numbers of Mexican employees—countered by insisting on the national need for unskilled labor, especially since the number of European immigrants had declined. Though the restrictionists achieved a reinforced border patrol, they failed to establish an immigration quota system for Mexico. The battle over Mexican immigration continued into the 1930s, but the issue became less pressing as the number of Mexicans entering the U.S. declined sharply because of the economic disruptions of the Great Depression. The Bureau of Immigration also appeased restrictionists by stepping up its efforts to deport illegal Mexican immigrants, especially those identified by cooperating welfare bureaus as "dependency problems."[14]

On the Eve of Depression

IN 1930, the Mexican Fact-Finding Committee of Governor C. C. Young reported that "Mexican immigrants have gained a strong foothold in California industries, undoubtedly supplanting other immigrant races and native Americans," and are "today a principal source of farm labor" working at "tasks white workers will not or cannot do."[15] Other reports also confirmed that Chicanos were among the poorest-paid groups in California. On the eve of the Great Depression their housing, diet, and wages placed them at society's lowest level. In the eyes of the public they were an "increasing" problem to be rid of, yet they provided the low-cost labor that harvested produce for markets, made the clothing sold in department stores, maintained the state's rail system, and performed many other essential tasks. Their barrios, especially in San Francisco, San Diego, San Jose, Riverside, Santa Barbara, and Los Angeles, constituted segregated "Mexican" cities within "American" cities. Indeed, by 1930 Los Angeles was the largest population center for Mexicans in the U.S., with well over a hundred thousand people.

The native-born and foreign-born Mexican residents of California in 1930 were over a generation removed from the experiences that had shaped the Mexican American reality of the late nineteenth century. Though society at large had changed and California had achieved steady — and often dramatic — economic development during the previous three decades, the material conditions of Chicanos had improved very little. Despite the dismal circumstances that characterized the vast majority of Mexican households, most Spanish-speaking Californians had made a commitment to stay. In truth, it was difficult for them to return to Mexico where political conditions were unstable and the Catholic Church was being persecuted. No doubt, most Mexican Californians hoped for a prosperous future in the U.S., but the ensuing decade of economic depression shattered their dreams and those of countless other Californians.

CHAPTER FOUR

Depression and Despair: 1930-1943

THE GREAT DEPRESSION is often regarded as a watershed in United States history. Like citizens everywhere in the nation, Californians suffered economic poverty, social deprivation, and much hopelessness. The psychological impact of the Great Depression was, perhaps, even more strongly felt in California than in other states because the spectacular economic growth of California abruptly halted. Thousands of jobless Americans migrated to the state during the 1930s in search of work and a mild climate, thus exacerbating the already glutted labor pool. They felt the disillusion and despair of unemployment and hunger, idleness and futility, and struggled to find relief from their distress.

For Chicanos in California the suffering of the depression also was disillusioning. Unlike most Californians, however, their experiences worsened significantly as a result of the federal government's massive deportation drives, the suppression of Chicano labor unions, and racial violence in the cities, which culminated in the so-called Zoot Suit Riots of 1943.

Depression and Deportation

T HE STOCK MARKET CRASH of 1929, the growing unemployment, and the bewildering uncertainty during the Great Depression seriously affected all Californians, but especially the poor and the ethnic minorities. Among the most vulnerable were Chicanos, a majority of whom were immigrants or descendants of recent immigrants who had come to the U.S. in search of work and refuge from the bloodshed and violence of the Mexican Revolution. Though they had contributed to the development of the state's manufacturing, agricultural, and service industries during the previous three decades, their status in society became increasingly precarious as prosperity turned to stagnation.

From the urban centers of San Francisco, Los Angeles, and San Diego to the rural agricultural valleys of Salinas, San Joaquin, and Imperial, Americans during the depression years expounded more loudly than ever before that refrain known as the "Mexican problem." Only now they redefined the "problem" in several ways: Mexicans were taking jobs away from American citizens who were already severely unemployed; Mexicans were disproportionately on welfare rolls and thus a serious drain on limited relief funds; and most Mexicans were illegally in the U.S. and should not benefit from public services intended for citizens alone. The problem related not only to Mexicans in California, but wherever they formed a visible minority in the nation. American authorities concluded that the solution lay in deporting Spanish-speaking individuals, making little or no attempt to distinguish between citizens and aliens. This program very quickly became a policy of *mass* deportation spearheaded by the U.S. Department of Labor and encouraged by President Herbert Hoover, who shared the popular conviction that Mexicans were taking jobs away from Americans. The Labor Department, in conjunction with welfare agencies and local governments, initiated efforts that between 1931 and 1933 resulted in the involuntary and voluntary repatriation of over 400,000 Mexicans and U.S. citizens of Mexican descent. Estimates of deportees from California alone range from 75,000 to 100,000.[1]

The most concerted repatriation efforts occurred in southern California. Sweeps there netted a high proportion of children who had been born in the U.S. and were thus American citizens. At first, federal and local officials tried to encourage voluntary repatriation. County welfare agencies, for example, often informed Mexicans on relief that unless they returned to Mexico of their own volition, they would be stricken from the welfare rolls. Federal immigration officers, with the aid of local media, either enticed Mexicans back to the homeland with exaggerated stories of government-sponsored colonization programs there or employed scare tactics, such as reports of widespread arrests of illegals by immigration authorities. Newspapers contributed to the anxiety among Mexicans by printing articles intended to frighten them into returning home. One such article, published by the *Los Angeles Times,* announced that the "U.S. and City Join in Drive on L.A. Aliens." The director of unemployment relief in Los Angeles, C. P. Visel, heightened the fears among local Mexicans by distributing leaflets in barrios which claimed that authorities would deport both legal and illegal immigrants. Rumors of impending arrests and deportation raids also spread apprehension. "Through a whispering rumor campaign which gathered strength as time went on . . . ," the District Director of Immigration wrote in 1931, "the Mexican population was led to believe, in many instances, that Mexicans were not wanted in California and that all would be deported whether they were legally here or not." News reports confirmed the pervasiveness of Mexican fears. According to the *New York Times* in 1931, "arrests by [immigration] agents have terrified the Mexicans. . . . They dread being sent to jail."[2]

Where voluntary repatriation did not succeed, forced deportation was used. Again, welfare agencies often played a key role by identifying Mexicans on the relief rolls for apprehension by immigration officers. On other occasions, immigration dragnets aimed at all Mexicans (regardless of citizenship) occurred at such popular places as movie theaters, dance halls, plazas, or job sites. One of the largest raids by immigration officers took place in 1931 in Placita Park, the downtown Los Angeles plaza frequented by Mexican families for many generations. Immigration agents and Los Angeles police officers surrounded and

questioned four hundred people in the old plaza area. "Indigna-
tion was reigning in the colonia [Mexican community]," the
Mexican vice-consul reported to his superiors in Mexico City,
because innocent persons were "subjected to public interroga-
tions in an angry and discourteous manner."[3]

For recent immigrants there was great apprehension about
making contact with anyone outside the barrios and colonias.
For those who had originally intended to return but had instead planted roots in American society—some for one, two, or
more decades—there was anxiety about losing what they had
achieved. Perhaps most terrified were the immigrants' children
who had been born and raised in California and who knew of
Mexico only through family stories and traditional observances.
Other family members experienced anxiety about relocating to
Mexico, especially the mothers who were in a double bind.
According to sociologist Emory Bogardus, who observed the
repatriations:

> The mother is in a dilemma. She wants to go back with her
> husband to Mexico but does not want to desert her older
> children, who beg to remain in the United States. She faces
> a divided family. She is pulled strongly in two different ways
> at the same time.[4]

In many cases the alarm proved warranted, since adjustment
to society and life in Mexico was often difficult even for the
returned native. A *corrido* (folk ballad) about repatriates re-
counts how residents of Mexico perceived the returnees:

> I shall sing you a song, of all who were deported
> Who came back speaking English from those wretches.
> They are shoved around anywhere and have to beg their way.
> It's a pity to see them with nothing to eat.[5]

Most *repatriados* returned to their native villages and towns
while a minority relocated in large cities.

The deportations touched nearly everyone in Chicano society,
leaving lasting memories among those who had left as well as
those who remained behind. Families were often separated for
long periods of time, and some were never reunited. Neighbors
were always aware of the families who had left the barrio,
voluntarily or by force, and returned to Mexico by train or car.
"I'll never forget as long as I live," recalled a Santa Barbara

woman, "[how] they put all the people that went in boxcars instead of inside the trains." "They were in here illegally," she explained, "but the moral part of it, like separation and putting them in boxcars," is what made the scene unforgettable. Tearful farewells of relatives and friends occurred weekly along the tracks at the Los Angeles railroad terminal as the county-sponsored trains departed for the interior of Mexico. Author Carey McWilliams witnessed the first trainload of repatriates leaving Union Station in Los Angeles in February 1931: "'Repatriados' arrived by the truckload—men, women, and children—with dogs, cats, and goats . . . half-open suitcases, rolls of bedding, and lunch baskets." Lucas Lucio, who helped organize his fellow countrymen in Los Angeles for the long trip home, observed sadly, "the majority of men were very quiet and pensive" and "most of the women and children were crying."[6] Repatriation experiences were preserved in bitter corridos:

> Now I go to my country
> Where although at times they make war
> They will not run us from there.
> Goodbye, my good friends,
> You are all witnesses
> Of the bad payment they give us.[7]

Yet the dismal economic situation of most Mexicans prompted them to take the chance of going back to Mexico—after all, many believed, the conditions in the homeland could not be any worse than in America.

The Chicano community did not passively accept the indignity heaped upon it by the governmental deportation drives. Organizations, such as the Comité de Beneficencia Mexicana in Los Angeles, and Spanish-language newspapers such as *La Opinión* and *El Heraldo* decried the tactics used by *la migra* (the immigration service) to encourage and force Mexicans to cross the border. Mexican consulate officers protested the indiscriminate apprehension of any person who "looked Mexican" regardless of citizenship and mobilized to protect the threatened communities. They also attempted to cushion the shock for those repatriates who volunteered to return by offering food or money for the trip south and by providing information about conditions in Mexico.[8]

Though the Mexican consulate, community organizations, and the Spanish-language press helped ameliorate the suffering caused by the deportation drives, they were unable to counter the powerful federal and local governmental forces. For Chicano communities in California and elsewhere in the U.S., the depression and the deportations demonstrated that Mexicans were an undesirable element and an expendable work force during "bad times."

Class Conflict in the Fields and Cities

D URING THE DEPRESSION, arrest and deportation became a common union-busting tactic of employers. Mexicans nevertheless participated in an unprecedented number of labor strikes. The wave of rural and urban strikes in California can be explained from both sides. Employers sought to maintain their profit margins by paying labor as little as possible, while employees protested the wage reductions and increasingly poor working conditions. For workers, there was relatively less at stake in the 1930s than earlier as the depression wiped out the little security they may have had. This situation was especially true for those who had fought in the Mexican Revolution and were willing to fight now for a better standard of living.

Though the agricultural labor conflicts of the depression years included Anglos as well as Filipinos and Japanese, a large percentage of the workers, and sometimes the majority, were Mexicans. Their attempts to unionize took a major step forward in 1930 with the reorganization of the Mexican Mutual Aid Society in the Imperial Valley. The subsequent strike of Mexican cantaloupe workers, like the earlier 1928 strike, ultimately failed because of the unwillingness of growers to negotiate and because the Mexican union was undermined by the Communist party's Trade Union Unity League (TUUL), which had recently decided to organize farm workers. TUUL formed the Agricultural Workers Industrial Union, which led several strikes in 1930 and 1931. In the latter year the union sought to broaden

The headquarters of the Cannery and Agricultural Workers Industrial Union during the 1933 San Joaquin Valley cotton pickers' strike. The signs are printed in Spanish only, reflecting the dominant influence of Mexican strikers. (*Reproduced through the courtesy of The Bancroft Library, University of California, Berkeley*)

its appeal to another large group of nonunionized workers by changing its name to the Cannery and Agricultural Workers Industrial Union (CAWIU). Two years later CAWIU emerged as the principal organizer of farm labor strikes in the state.[9]

CAWIU directed most of the thirty-seven major strikes called in 1933, a year of unprecedented labor activity in California, when economic conditions were at their worst. Striking for better wages took courage as some fifty thousand workers walked off their jobs. The strike in the San Joaquin Valley alone kept eighteen thousand cotton pickers out of the fields, while the El Monte berry strike, the Imperial Valley lettuce strike, the Sunnyvale cherry strike, the Fresno grape strike, and the Santa Clara Valley cannery strike idled additional thousands of workers. CAWIU did not initiate all the strikes of 1933 and after, but it became involved in virtually every labor dispute and in some cases won slight wage increases for workers. Major successes

The tent city of striking cotton pickers in Corcoran during the 1933 San Joaquin Valley strike (notice the stage of the Circo Azteca on the left), a large majority of whom were Mexican. (*Reproduced through the courtesy of The Bancroft Library, University of California, Berkeley*)

proved elusive because of glutted markets and the large numbers of unemployed willing to step into jobs vacated by strikers. An additional restraint was the violent reaction of grower vigilantes, sheriffs' deputies, and local police against the "Red" organizers of the union. Such repressive tactics slowed and then stilled the union's organizing efforts. By 1935 CAWIU was broken, and its leaders were being prosecuted under California's criminal syndicalism law.

While CAWIU was under attack by authorities, Mexican workers in 1933 created a new union in southern California, La Confederación de Uniones de Campesinos y Obreros Mexicanos (CUCOM). CUCOM represented a reorganization of a confederation of Mexican mutual aid societies originally formed in 1928 under the banner of La Confederación de Uniones Obreras Mexicanas. Under the leadership of a small group of unionists and the Mexican vice-consul of Los Angeles, CUCOM quickly grew to a membership of some ten thousand workers, fifteen hundred of whom went on strike in 1933 in the El Monte berry fields. The wage increases achieved by the berry strike, though less than what CUCOM leaders had wanted, still represented a victory and led to other successful strikes in 1934 and 1935. Eventually resistance from powerful grower groups—"farm fascism" as Carey McWilliams described it—prompted CUCOM to create alliances with other unions.[10]

In 1936 CUCOM joined with labor leaders from the Filipino and Japanese communities to establish the Federation of Agricultural Workers Unions of America (FAWUA). This organization hoped to create a number of AFL locals which would then merge into a state organization of farm workers, a scheme that never came to fruition. In 1936 the FAWUA called several strikes in Los Angeles and Orange counties over low wages and poor working conditions. Armed guards of the Associated Farmers, the state's most powerful grower organization, then launched what the *Los Angeles Examiner* described as "open private warfare" against the strikers. Growers branded the FAWUA leadership, like the CAWIU before it, as Communist and encouraged authorities to rout the union with whatever tactics seemed necessary. The resulting beatings, tear-gassings, and arrests caused the FAWUA-led strikes to collapse.[11]

The efforts of FAWUA, CUCOM, and other unions to acquire

AFL recognition never materialized because of dissension within the AFL over organization and tactics. Though some AFL officials favored organization of farm workers, the principal leaders of the union resisted. This issue as well as other disagreements led in 1937 to the formation of a splinter group, the Congress of Industrial Organizations (CIO). During the following year, a former AFL leader, Donald Henderson, helped create and then headed the CIO's United Cannery, Agricultural, Packing, and Allied Workers of America (UCAPAWA). This national labor union attracted most of the Mexican agriculture-related unions in California and became the spearhead of the farm labor movement during the late 1930s.

Initially, UCAPAWA achieved great success among agricultural and cannery workers throughout the nation. After only eighteen months, it boasted over 300 locals and some 125,000 dues-paying members. By 1939 it had become the seventh largest CIO union and had attracted the support of influential politicians. UCAPAWA seemed to be on the way to becoming *the* union for agricultural workers when it ran into major obstacles. In California the usual difficulties of organizing a geographically mobile, seasonal farm labor force worsened dramatically with the arrival of the Dust Bowl refugees, who further glutted the labor pool. The effects of the National Labor Relations Act of 1935, which had not covered agricultural workers, and increased harassment and deportation of alleged Communist organizers in the union were other setbacks. In 1940 the weakened UCAPAWA limited its efforts to cannery and packing-shed workers, and four years later formally changed its name to the Food, Tobacco, and Allied Workers to reflect the new emphasis. UCAPAWA recorded some victories during the 1940s, but the rise of anti-Communist hysteria threatened the union's left-oriented leadership and forced many of its most capable organizers, such as the dynamic Luisa Moreno who served as vice president and organizer of UCAPAWA's California locals, to resign from the union.[12]

UCAPAWA had been one of the few labor unions to organize Mexican and other agricultural workers in both rural and urban areas. It had also been one of the few unions in which women held positions of leadership. Its efforts to unionize female cannery workers represented a new and important step in the organization of the Mexican American working class.

Among other significant attempts to organize urban Chicano workers during the depression was the strike of the International Ladies' Garment Workers' Union in 1933 against Los Angeles dress factories. (About seventy-five percent of the employees were Mexican women.) Though the ILGWU had only limited success, its accomplishments included a minimum wage scale and tacit recognition by employers. Most importantly, the strike introduced unionization to Mexican women workers in an industry known for its sweatshops and exploitation. [13]

Headquarters of striking ILGWU members, located in east Los Angeles, circa 1940. (*Courtesy of Margaret Garb Lehman*)

Political and Community Organizations

THE LABOR UNION MOVEMENT of the 1930s played a pivotal role in politicizing Mexican workers in the cities and towns. The most significant civil rights organization of the period, El Congreso de Pueblos de Habla Española (Congress of Spanish Speaking People), emerged partly as a spin-off of unionization efforts and partly as a result of the contact already established among Mexican mutual aid societies in southern California.

The inspiration and foresight which led to the formation of the Congreso belonged primarily to Luisa Moreno. A native of Guatemala, she immigrated to the U.S. in 1928 with her Mexican husband after having spent two years in Mexico City as a correspondent for a Guatemalan newspaper. Though she intended to pursue a career as a poet, she discovered that she could not earn a living and turned to work as a seamstress in a garment factory near Spanish Harlem. There she labored for meager wages to support her unemployed husband and infant daughter. The sweatshop environment in which she worked and the appalling living conditions of Latinos in New York led to her radicalization. "Hunger is the best teacher," she later observed.

Moreno joined El Central Obrero de Habla Español, a group of left-wing Puerto Ricans, Cubans, and Mexicans who persuaded her to become a labor organizer. She first worked among Puerto Rican women garment workers in Spanish Harlem and participated in the 1933 strike of the Needle Trades Workers Industrial Union, which later merged with the International Ladies' Garment Workers' Union. When the ILGWU weakened in its resolve to organize Spanish-speaking women, Moreno in 1935 joined the AFL as a professional organizer. Assigned to work in Florida among cigar makers, she soon had a falling out with her superiors over their handling of contract negotiations. She was reassigned to Pennsylvania and then, in 1937, thoroughly dissatisfied with the lack of support of AFL officials, she split with the union and joined John L. Lewis and other disenchanted AFL leaders who formed the CIO. She then helped

Striking garment workers picketing a coat and suit manufacturer in downtown Los Angeles, circa 1940. Philip Garb (in long coat), organizer for the International Ladies' Garment Workers' Union, led Chicano and other garment workers in this strike over employer violations of laws governing employee wages and hours and the firing of union members. (*Courtesy of Margaret Garb Lehman*)

organize cigar industry workers in New York City, Philadelphia, and Lancaster. During this early phase of her career, Moreno, an avid reader, discovered the writings of Paul S. Taylor, an economics professor at the University of California, Berkeley, who had written extensively about Mexican labor in the U.S. "He was my teacher," she recalled. Alarmed by Taylor's descriptions of the plight of Mexican workers in Texas, she traveled to San Antonio where pecan shellers were in the midst of a bitter strike against employers. "The conditions and discrimination against Mexicans," she remembered, "were worse than Paul Taylor had described." Shortly after her arrival she became an organizer with the United Cannery, Agricultural, Packing, and Allied Workers of America.[14]

Luisa Moreno, union leader of the CIO's United Cannery, Agricultural, Packing, and Allied Workers of America (UCAPAWA) and principal organizer in the Congreso de Pueblos de Habla Española, circa 1940. (*Courtesy of Bert Corona*)

Moreno's work with the pecan shellers convinced her that if unionization were to succeed, it had to proceed hand-in-hand with the protection of civil rights. "You could not organize workers in the face of violence and terror," she concluded. Her solution was to argue for the creation of a national organization that would provide strength by unifying Mexican and other Spanish-speaking workers across the U.S. The quickest way to achieve such unity, she believed, lay in establishing a confedera-tion of existing local organizations. In 1938 she took a leave of absence from her union responsibilities and organized the first national meetings of the Congress of Spanish Speaking People. Held in Los Angeles in 1939, the Congress attracted not only Chicanos, who made up the large majority of those in attendance, but also other Spanish-speaking groups, particularly Puerto Ricans and Cubans. Mutual aid association officers, students, educators, and workers were among the fifteen hundred in attendance. Present also were such dignitaries as California lieutenant governor Ellis Patterson, emissaries from Mexico, and representatives from major national labor unions.

"The guiding genius of the Congreso was Luisa Moreno," recalled Bert Corona, long-time labor and community organizer in California and original member of the Congress. But the meeting also allowed others to move into positions of leadership. Among them were Eduardo Quevedo, Sr., and Josephine Fierro de Bright whom the delegates elected president and executive secretary, respectively. Corona found them all unusually impressive.

> Quevedo was a very, very forceful and very brilliant leader. . . . He was a tremendous spokesman — very competent, very charismatic, very excellent speaker, as well as dedicated organizer and grass roots worker. He had spent most of his life . . . working in the mines, working on the railroad tracks, working in the packing sheds. He understood the problems of workers and he was very familiar with the labor union struggles. . . . And he understood very well the dynamic operations of confederations and how you have to build cohesiveness among groups that had different bases and maybe different local interests, but the same national interests.

Josephine Fierro de Bright "was very dynamic, also very charismatic, and an excellent speaker," Corona remembered, "very natural as an organizer."

> As a child she had traveled up and down the state and the Southwest following the crops. Her mother and her family had followed the crops, living with the farm workers. Her mother had been with Flores Magón, leader of the anti–Porfirio Díaz organization, Partido Liberal Mexicano, which operated in Los Angeles after banishment from Mexico in 1904. . . . She was also a natural organizer. . . . She knew the Southwest, she knew the various occupations and problems of

Mexican workers and their families, not only in agriculture but in nonagricultural industrial areas.[15]

Fierro de Bright also brought financial support from Hollywood liberals whom she knew through her husband, screenwriter John Bright.

Josephine Fierro de Bright, first national secretary of the Congreso de Pueblos de Habla Española, circa 1940. (*Courtesy of Bert Corona*)

Los Angeles headquarters and leaders of the California chapter of the Congreso de Pueblos de Habla Española, circa 1940. (*Courtesy of Bert Corona*)

The three-day meeting of the Congreso focused on such questions as work, health, education, racial prejudice, equality for women, and the problems of Latin American youth. The deliberations ended with resolutions calling for adequate housing and health care, a Spanish-language newspaper to aid in the organization and education of Latino trade unionists, more government relief to unemployed workers, a congressional investigation of the substandard conditions of the Mexican population, elimination of racial discrimination, and protection of civil rights.[16] As the first national civil rights organization for Chicanos and other Spanish-speaking groups, the Congreso represented a significant achievement and foreshadowed similar Chicano organizations of the 1960s and 1970s. The leadership roles of women such as Moreno and Fierro de Bright also set it apart from most other groups.

The Congreso soon fell on hard times, however. Because its ranks did not include elected public officials, it lacked sufficient clout to translate its resolutions into policies or legislation. Other difficulties arose because some of its leaders came from radical labor organizations and the Communist party. They attracted opposition from the news media, the House Committee on Un-American Activities, and the FBI. Lack of funds and the onset of World War II—which resulted in the induction of many Chicano leaders—only added to the problems. By the end of the war, the Congress of Spanish Speaking People existed little more than in name. [17]

Before its demise the Congreso promoted the development of numerous local organizations across the Southwest—especially in California—and as far north as Chicago, dedicated to improving the socioeconomic status of Chicanos. Among its successful activities were regional youth conferences, some of which fed into the establishment of the Mexican American Movement (MAM). MAM evolved from a YMCA barrio club and became the first student organization in Los Angeles to promote education for barrio youth and to publicize the problems facing Chicanos in the school system. Its chief objective was "to encourage and inspire higher education achievements among our Mexican-American people as a means of overcoming the problems of prejudice, segregation, discrimination, social inequality, and inferiority complexes." Like the Congreso, MAM lost its vitality during the early 1940s as many of its young leaders left for military service. [18]

Contrary to the stereotypic characterization of Mexican Americans in popular and scholarly literature of this period, Chicanos were not a passive, apolitical people lacking organizational abilities. They continued their heritage of building community, political, and labor organizations wherever they settled. Still, the effects of the war years and the economic and racial obstacles that they encountered prevented them from developing organizations of lasting significance.

Pachuquismo, Sleepy Lagoon, and the Zoot Suit Riots

NOTHING HAS COME to symbolize more dramatically the racial hostility encountered by Chicanos during the 1930s and 1940s than the Sleepy Lagoon case and the Zoot Suit Riots. Both involved Chicano youth in Los Angeles city and county, local police departments, and the judicial system.

At the heart of these conflicts was the growing attention paid to Chicano youth by the local media. The press focused on *pachucos,* members of local clubs or neighborhood gangs of teen-agers (both male and female). They separated themselves from other barrio youth by their appearance—high-pompadoured ducktail haircuts, tattoos, and baggy zoot suits for boys; short skirts, bobby sox, and heavy make-up for girls—and by their use of *caló,* a mixture of Spanish and English. Their charac-teristics, according to the press, included unflinching allegiance to neighborhood territories, clannishness, and bravado. Though other teenagers in cities such as Detroit, Chicago, and New York dressed like their counterparts in wartime Los Angeles, *pachuquismo* became popularly identified with Chicano youth who came of age during the 1930s and 1940s in the Los Ange-les area. Predominantly children of immigrant parents, these youths matured in an environment in which they saw them-selves as neither fully Mexican nor American. Raised in impov-erished barrios and alienated from a society that discriminated against Mexicans, they identified only with others of their age and experience. Pachucos constituted a minority among Chi-cano youth, and they set themselves apart by their disdain of the public schools, skipping classes and drawing together into neighborhood gangs where they found companionship and camaraderie. To outsiders who relied on the local media for their information, pachucos were perceived not only as marijuana-smoking hoodlums and violence-prone deviants, but also as un-American. These stigmas during the early 1940s, particu-larly during the first two years of a frustrating war for Ameri-cans, helped create a climate of repression for pachucos and, by extension, to others in the Chicano community.[19]

In the hot summer days of August 1942, most Los Angeles

residents had wearied of newspaper reports of setbacks against
the Japanese forces in the Pacific. Japanese Americans on the
home front had already been relocated to internment camps,
thereby temporarily silencing Californians embittered by Pearl
Harbor. Many xenophobic citizens also did not like Mexicans,
especially the "foreign, different-looking" pachucos arrested following an incident at Sleepy Lagoon.

Sleepy Lagoon, a swimming hole frequented by Chicano
youth of east Los Angeles, soon became the symbol of both
popular outrage and repression. At a home near the lagoon,
where the night before two rival gangs had confronted one
another, the body of a young Chicano was discovered. Though
no evidence indicated murder, the Los Angeles Police Department summarily arrested members of the 38th Street Club, the
teenage group that had crashed a party the prior evening and
precipitated the fighting.

The grand jury indicted twenty-two members of the club
for murder and, according to Carey McWilliams, "to fantastic
orchestration of 'crime' and 'mystery' provided by the Los Angeles press seventeen of the youngsters were convicted in what
was, up to that time, the largest mass trial for murder ever held
in the country." Reflecting on the treatment of the Sleepy
Lagoon defendants, the aroused McWilliams stated:

> For years, Mexicans had been pushed around by the Los Ange-
> les police and given a very rough time in the courts, but the
> Sleepy Lagoon prosecution capped the climax. It took place
> before a biased and prejudiced judge (found to be such by an
> appellate court); it was conducted by a prosecutor who pointed
> to the clothes and the style of haircut of the defendants as
> evidence of guilt; and was staged in an atmosphere of intense
> community-wide prejudice which had been whipped up and
> artfully sustained by the entire press of Los Angeles. . . . From
> the beginning the proceedings savored more of a ceremonial
> lynching than a trial in a court of justice.[20]

Concerned Anglo and Chicano citizens, headed by McWilliams,
sharply criticized violations of the defendants' constitutional
and human rights (such as beatings by police while the youths
were being held incommunicado and the courtroom impropri-
eties indicated above by McWilliams). They organized the
Sleepy Lagoon Defense Committee and, with the support of

such groups as the Congreso and UCAPAWA, faced down intimidation by the media and accusations of being "reds" by state
senator Jack Tenney and his Committee on Un-American Activities. In 1944 they succeeded in persuading the District
Court of Appeals to reverse the convictions, declare a mistrial,
and release the defendants from San Quentin prison.[21]

The Sleepy Lagoon case served as a prelude to an even more
discriminatory episode in wartime Los Angeles—the so-called
Zoot Suit Riots of 1943. Racial tensions intensified after the
Sleepy Lagoon case as police continued to arrest large numbers
of Chicano youth on a variety of charges. Adding to the unrest
were confrontations between military servicemen and Chicano
zoot suiters on city streets. Then on June 3, 1943, rumors
circulated that Chicanos had beaten sailors over an incident
involving some young Mexican women. The newspapers seized
on the rumor and soon sailors and marines from nearby bases
converged on the downtown area and on Chicano neighborhoods. There they attacked Chicano youth, regardless of whether
they wore zoot suits, beat them, stripped off their clothes, and
left them to be arrested by the police who did nothing to
interfere with the "military operations." A virtual state of siege
existed for Chicanos in Los Angeles as hundreds of servicemen
in "taxicab brigades" looked for Mexicans on whom to vent
their anger. "I never believed that I could see a thing like that,"
recalled Josephine Fierro de Bright.

> I went downtown and my husband and I were standing there
> and we saw all these policemen hanging around . . . and hun-
> dreds of taxis with sailors hanging on with clubs in their
> hands, bullies just beating Mexicans on Main Street. And we
> went up and asked a cop to stop it : he says, "You better shut
> up or I'll do the same to you." You can't do a thing when you
> see people and the ambulances coming to pick them up and
> nobody is stopping the slaughter. It's a nightmare. It's a ter-
> rible thing to see.[22]

The local press continued to feed the hysteria with headlines
announcing the sailors' "war" against zoot-suited pachucos.
After five days of beatings, mass arrests, and rampant fear in
Chicano communities, military authorities—ordered by federal
officials at the request of the Mexican consulate—quelled the

riots by declaring downtown Los Angeles off limits to all naval personnel.[23]

In the wake of the riots, which also occurred in San Diego and several other communities but with much less violence than in Los Angeles, the Chicano community remained paralyzed with fear of another occurrence. The Mexican government and many local citizens protested the outrages, and Governor Earl Warren appointed a committee composed of clergy, public officials, and other well-known citizens to investigate the incident. Even so, Chicano relations with the police remained tense for many years. Jesse Saldana, a Los Angeles resident who witnessed the riots, articulated the sentiment of many Chicanos: "Justice is blind, she can't see the Mexicans."[24]

The Zoot Suit Riots climaxed an era of overt hostility against Chicanos in California. Beginning with mass deportations during the early years of the depression and the violent suppression of unionization efforts, the 1930s and early 1940s witnessed much sadness and frustration for Chicanos who struggled to keep family and neighborhood from moral and physical deterioration. The irony was that tens of thousands of Mexican fathers and sons were fighting overseas with the U.S. armed forces as their families on the home front were experiencing bigotry and persecution. But this period of depression and repression also aroused in Chicanos a desire to gain the equality that eluded them. The post–World War II decades witnessed a new upsurge of activity and a sense of hope within the Mexican community.

CHAPTER FIVE

Progress and Disappointment— World War II and After: 1941–1960

T HE SECOND WORLD WAR and the years immediately following were a pivotal period for Chicanos in California. The war effort at home and abroad kindled in everyone, and Chicanos were no exception, a sense of patriotism and commitment to American democratic ideals. For returning Chicano G.I.s, these feelings were manifested in a determination to bring themselves and their families into the mainstream of American society. After all, thousands of young Mexican Americans had risked and given their lives to defend the nation, and they believed Chicanos now deserved the same opportunities as Anglo Americans. This conviction took the form of new community organizations, movement into better kinds of jobs, and a growing middle class. Advances came slowly and were accompanied often by disappointing setbacks, but they established the basis for the Chicano civil rights movement of the 1960s.

The Effects of War

THE ATTACK ON PEARL HARBOR of December 7, 1941, shocked Americans and most other peoples around the world. The ensuing mobilization and years of war affected every U.S. citizen regardless of where he or she lived—in the congested neighborhoods of metropolitan New York or on the open farmlands of California's central valley. The war effort forced young men to enlist or face the draft, and it left families and friends separated, some for several years and others forever. From everywhere in California—farms, towns, and cities—young men went first to training centers and then overseas.

Mobilization affected American men in common ways. Many enlisted for patriotic reasons, but most were drafted into service. Regardless of how they entered the military, the great majority experienced for the first time the sorrow of leaving their home town. Like other Americans, Chicano recruits went to boot camps in California and elsewhere in the Southwest and sometimes as far away as South Carolina and Georgia. The experience of being away from insulated Chicano neighborhoods had a profound effect on their lives. It was the first opportunity for most to observe the regional and state differences that existed in such a vast country. It was also for many their first experience with blatant racism even though segregation and discrimination existed in their home communities, ofttimes in subtle ways that were not always obvious to young Chicanos. Carlos López, a resident of San Jose, experienced his first example of overt discrimination during his army service from 1945 to 1947. "The only time I did see it [discrimination]," he remembered, "was when I was in the service. . . . We were in Wichita, Kansas, and we were refused service in a restaurant just because we were Mexican." [1]

Chicano soldiers in the combat zones faced a different kind of discrimination. Assignment of Chicanos to the infantry regardless of their aptitude test scores became routine. Raul Morín was especially blunt in describing his thoughts before his first battle in the European theatre: "Why fight for America when you have not been treated as an American?" "Can't you see," he pondered, "that they are only using you for the dirtiest and most dangerous of all branches [the infantry]?" [2]

Assignment to the infantry, according to Larry Amaya of Los Angeles, an ex-G.I. who helped establish organizations for Chicano war veterans, was often accompanied by assignment to the most hazardous combat duties—such as scout or point man or automatic rifleman. Officers found it easy to exploit the sense of *machismo,* or supermanliness, of Latin American males. Many Mexican American G.I.s volunteered for hazardous duties, exhibiting an exaggerated patriotism produced by their determination to prove that they were as "American" as anyone. Among the most popular Chicano songs of the period was "Soldado Razo":

> I leave as a common soldier, I'm going to join the ranks. I will be among the brave boys. . . . I'm leaving for the war contented. I have my rifle and gun ready. . . . And so hereforth goes another Mexican who is willing to gamble his life. And I say goodbye with this song. . . . Long live this country of mine.[3]

The military experience gave Chicano servicemen unusual opportunities to see other cities where large concentrations of Mexicans resided and to share in the camaraderie among Mexican Americans from different backgrounds. "The gathering of so many from different sections," Raul Morín wrote in his book on Mexican American participation in World War II, "afforded the Spanish-speaking people living in the United States a valuable and much-needed opportunity to study and improve their social life." "Here for the first time," he noted, "they had an opportunity to observe, compare, and personally get to know many others of our ethnic group and what they were like." Cultural and linguistic diversity and similarity were readily evident. Those from east Los Angeles usually spoke more English and at a faster pace than those from Texas and New Mexico. The barrio slang, caló, was often used by young Chicanos from El Paso or Los Angeles, but was something new to recruits born and raised in Gary, Indiana, or Kansas City, Kansas. Native-born Mexican Americans—many of whom were descendants of the original colonizers of the borderlands—were naturally more acculturated to American popular culture (music, food, dress, and language) than their counterparts who had immigrated from Mexico. Chicanos from the Midwest typically spoke less

Spanish and came from communities where Mexicans were a small minority. Despite such differences, most recruits identified as Mexican Americans, tied as they were by language, folkways, and religion emanating from Mexico. Whether they called themselves Hispano (mostly those from New Mexico), Spanish-American, Latin American, Mexicano, Latino, or Chicano, all recognized the common bonds as well as the heterogeneity of Mexican American society.[4]

Chicanos distinguished themselves on the battlefields of North Africa, the beaches at Normandy and in the South Pacific, the icy wastelands of the Aleutian Islands, and in nearly every major campaign of the war. The heroes of Mexican descent were numerous, their bravery exemplified by their being the most decorated ethnic group of World War II.[5] Many of the medals of valor granted to Chicanos were awarded posthumously. There was a disproportionate number of Mexican American casualties relative to the group's percentage of the total population. Though Mexicans of Los Angeles, for example, accounted for approximately ten percent of the city's total population, they accounted for about twenty percent of the Angelenos killed in action. Losses were especially high in such "all Chicano companies" as Company E of the 141st Regiment of the 36th (Texas) division where all but twenty-three of the soldiers were killed in the Mediterranean campaigns. "Nearly all of the guys that I knew were killed or wounded," recalled Larry Amaya sadly. While Raul Morín was recuperating from wounds at De Witt General Hospital in northern California, he noted that "the place was full of Mexican-Americans" recovering from their injuries.[6]

On the Home Front

C HICANO G.I.s felt the impact of the war on their lives, but few realized its influence on those at home, especially the Mexican women in the urban centers. Though Chicanas in large numbers had long worked outside the home, they now moved in unprecedented numbers into industrial, manufacturing, and office jobs. As the manpower shortage developed, Chicanas,

Table 3 : Chicano Occupational Distribution in California,
1930–1970, by Sex (Percent)

Occupational Level	1930 M	1930 F	1950 M	1950 F	1960 M	1960 F	1970 M	1970 F
Professional & technical	1.0	3.0	2.6	4.7	4.5	5.2	6.5	7.2
Managers, proprietors & officials	1.9	1.8	4.5	3.5	4.2	2.3	4.9	2.3
Clerical	3.2	13.6	6.4	23.7	4.8	24.2	6.7	29.2
Sales					3.2	6.0	3.7	5.5
Craftsmen & Foremen (skilled)	7.0	1.4	13.9	1.8	16.6	1.5	20.4	2.3
Operatives (semiskilled)	8.1	40.8	21.6	41.2	24.4	32.4	26.9	27.9
Laborers (unskilled)	37.6	4.7	17.7	1.6	13.0	1.2	11.0	1.4
Service	4.2	27.5	5.5	16.9	6.5	16.8	10.8	20.3
Farm laborers	35.7	7.1	23.4	5.1	15.9	3.1	8.4	3.9
Farmers & farm managers	1.3	.1	2.7	.2	1.9	.1	.4	.1
Occupation not reported	—	—	0.0	1.3	6.3	7.1	—	—

Source : Mario Barrera, *Race and Class in the Southwest,* p. 136.

like American women everywhere, filled the labor gaps. War-
related employment as factory workers and other nontraditional
jobs, especially clerical positions, became available to many
Mexican women. This opportunity to work outside the home
offered them a new sense of independence and importance.

As Chicanas entered the war-related labor market, so did
many men who remained at home. Both encountered avenues of
occupational mobility denied earlier. Men left unskilled work
for semiskilled and skilled jobs and also joined local chapters of
national labor unions. By 1950, the percentage of California
Chicanos in semiskilled work had increased significantly as had
the percentage of skilled craftsmen and foremen (see Table 3).
Many Chicanos now worked as welders, plumbers, and riveters
in the shipyards and aircraft plants, as cement finishers and
plasterers at military installations, as machinists and boiler-
makers in the factories, and as mechanics and production-line

workers in munition plants. For many Chicano men and women on the home front there was a greater sense than before of opportunity and equality in participating in the fight for freedom and preservation of American democracy.[7]

War mobilization did not always redound to the benefit of Chicanos. As some gained admittance to major AFL craft unions, others, especially those in leadership positions in certain AFL and CIO-affiliated labor union locals (particularly those noted below) suffered serious setbacks. Perceived as "Communist dominated" and as unpatriotic, these union leaders fought unsuccessfully against discrimination in the hiring of minorities and women. Some helped found the Committee to Aid Mexican Workers and the California CIO Committee on Minorities, while others channeled complaints through the Fair Employment Practices Commission. These moves brought attempts to purge the "Communist front" locals from the national unions, investigations by the state's Tenney Committee on Un-American Activities, and harassment by U.S. immigration authorities who threatened many leaders with deportation. In numerous instances, the threats were carried out. Among those deported were Armando Davila of the United Furniture Workers Local 576, Luisa Moreno of UCAPAWA, Frank Corona of the shoe workers' union, and Frank Martínez of the Laborers' Union of San Diego. Likewise, several leaders of the Congreso were either deported or facing deportation by the end of the war. With so many leaders under attack or deported, the labor and civil rights movement for Chicanos had lost much of its earlier vitality by the end of the war. Another negative effect on community and labor organizations was the induction of many leaders into the armed forces. The absence of many such leaders was temporary, but the loss of others — for example, Ismael "Smiley" Rincón of Los Angeles, who had headed the Congreso's Committee on Youth and who was killed in action — was permanent and severe.[8]

Braceros

THE MOVE OF CHICANOS into new sectors of the California economy during the war accompanied the arrival of another group of Mexican workers, the *braceros* (literally, those who worked with their arms). Labor shortages in agriculture prompted the federal government in 1942 to arrange with Mexico for a supply of temporary workers. This so-called Bracero Program allowed workers under contract to American growers to enter the country and receive housing, minimum wages, protection against discrimination, and free round-trip transportation. The federal government regulated the program, but found the provisions difficult to enforce, and some braceros were exploited. The government did succeed in providing the desired labor, however. During the war years, over 150,000 braceros worked not only on U.S. farms, but also for railroads, and some even worked in urban industries.[9]

Though the Bracero Program was intended as a wartime emergency measure, U.S. agribusiness and other employers lobbied to keep it alive during the postwar years. In the 1950s the number of braceros dramatically increased as the program became nearly institutionalized under Public Law 78, enacted in 1951. During the next decade an average of 336,000 Mexican workers were recruited yearly under the law. Certain groups in Mexico—such as labor unions, which resented the maltreatment of braceros by Americans, and agricultural and industrial interests, which wanted a larger labor supply of their own—contested the agreement, but the Mexican government favored its continuance because the national economy had become dependent on the millions of dollars braceros funneled into the country. In 1964, however, some U.S. labor unions, politicians, and Chicano leaders joined with many Mexican government officials, who were embarrassed by the reports of violations of contract agreements and exploitation of their compatriots in the U.S., and pressed for the termination of Public Law 78. Such pressure, coming at the height of the civil rights movement, caused Congress to allow the Bracero Program to lapse at the end of the year.[10]

Thousands of braceros, however, never returned to their

homeland. Those who married U.S. citizens and those who remained without legal documents were part of a process that predated the twentieth century. But braceros differed from previous migrations of Mexicans to the borderlands because they had arrived with government sanction and without wives and families. Their arrival also tended to obscure other changes in the historic migration patterns of Mexicans within the U.S. A major population shift of Chicanos during the war and postwar years was rural-to-urban, and it consisted of both undocumented migrants from Mexico and internal migration of the native-born. This process had actually been in motion for over thirty years, but it now dramatically intensified.

Urbanization and Rural-to-Urban Migration

DURING THE FIRST THREE DECADES of the twentieth century Mexican immigrants increasingly settled in southwestern cities, and by the time of the Great Depression, over half of the Mexican-origin population in the U.S. resided in urban locales. In 1930, sixty-six percent of the Mexicans in California were living in cities, while in Texas (the second most highly urbanized state for Chicanos) the percentage was forty-seven, with New Mexico and Arizona lagging far behind. A majority of these Mexicans inhabited the larger metropolitan centers throughout the region. In California, the cities of Los Angeles, San Diego, San Bernardino, and Santa Barbara accounted for almost a third of the state's Mexican population in 1930.[11]

The immigrants to California's cities, especially those relocating from an agricultural/pastoral village, had to make major adjustments in their life styles. The hacienda, rancho, or small pueblo was replaced by the ethnic enclave in a neighborhood somewhat familiar, yet foreign. Rural Mexico's cornfields, adobes, and burros gave way to urban barrios within concrete and steel cities. The transition was often an emotional experience softened somewhat by scenes reminiscent of the mother country—Sunday church services, vegetable gardens, cockfights, and a variety of customs associated with birth, marriage, and death. For urban Mexican immigrants the adaptation, while much less difficult because of their prior experience with city life, was also stressful.

Whether from urban or rural areas in Mexico, immigrants quickly borrowed elements from their American surroundings. Strong forces of assimilation were particularly prevalent in the cities, where English words crept into Mexican conversations, particularly among the first-generation children born in the U.S. Styles of dress, some American foods, and the dominant societal institutions—such as the schools, churches, and public agencies—all left an impact on the lives of the Mexican Americans. Some Mexicans intermarried, others joined Protestant churches, and many bought automobiles which allowed them to leave the barrio for work and recreation. The longer that Mexican immigrants remained in the U.S. the more they, and especially their native-born children, put aside the language and folkways of Mexico.

The rural-to-urban migration of American-born Chicanos from other states in the Southwest also significantly increased from the 1920s to the 1940s. "The twenties brought a substantial internal redistribution of the Chicano population," according to demographer Marta Tienda, and California once again received "its share of the total Mexican-origin population while Texas and Colorado experienced relative declines." [12] Thousands of newcomers to California cities had been migrant agricultural laborers in Texas or small farmers and ranchers in New Mexico. Most of the latter had been forced off their ancestral lands because of their inability to compete with agribusiness and corporate cattle interests which monopolized the lands managed by the U.S. Forest Service. Spanish-speaking villagers and ranchers from northern New Mexico found themselves dispossessed of their property by foreclosure because they could not meet payments on their mortgages or no longer could eke out a subsistence on their small plots of land. Uprooted and homeless, they and their families moved to West Coast cities, a migration that began as early as the economic depression following World War I which worsened in the 1920s for farmers and then nosedived precipitously during the Great Depression.

Because of the Works Progress Administration and other federal
employment and relief programs, opportunities in the urban
areas, while few, were far greater than in the country. At the
same time, urban Anglos were seeking homes in the suburbs of
the metropolitan areas. As Anglos moved from the inner cities,
Chicanos and blacks took their places. After 1940 Chicanos
throughout the Southwest headed for the cities in greater volume than ever before in their search for the better-paying jobs
spawned by California's expanded war economy. This attraction
remained in the postwar years. During the 1950s, California
received almost sixty percent of all Mexican Americans who
moved from other states in the Southwest; Texas was second
with only seventeen percent. Chicanos from Texas formed a
large part of the population that resettled in California's cities.
"We came to California," remarked a Chicana migrant farm
worker who left Texas in 1940, "waiting and hoping to find a
better living, a better living condition for ourselves and our
family." [13] This movement to California from Mexico and away
from Texas reversed a traditional pattern and continues into the
1980s.

Throughout the Southwest, but particularly in California,
Chicanos constituted the most rapidly urbanizing group. By
1950 urban Chicanos accounted for sixty-six percent of the total
Mexican-origin population in the Southwest (seventy-six percent in California). Within ten years that percentage increased
to seventy-nine. Most migrants headed for four California metropolitan areas—Los Angeles, San Francisco, San Bernardino, and
San Jose—where the Chicano population in 1960 ranged from
over 600,000 in greater Los Angeles to about 75,000 in metropolitan San Jose. [14]

Opportunities and Barriers
after the War

THE VICTORY OF THE U.S. in defense of American democracy during the Second World War inspired most Chicano
veterans and nonveterans, women as well as men, with a new
sense of hope. Many channeled this enthusiasm into organiza-

tional and political activities. War veteran Raul Morín, returning to Los Angeles after a long recuperation period in an army
hospital, expressed sentiments shared by other Chicano veterans.

> For too long we had been like outsiders. It had never made
> very much difference to us and we hardly noticed it until we
> got back from overseas. How could we have played such a
> prominent role as Americans over there and now have to go
> back living as outsiders again? How long had we been miss-
> ing out on benefits derived as an American citizen? Oldtimers
> had told us and we had read in books how the early settlers had
> invaded our towns and had shoved us into the "other side of
> the tracks." But we, ourselves, had never made much attempt
> to move out of there. The towns had grown up, population
> had increased, State, County, and City and community gov-
> ernment had been set up and we had been left out of it. We
> never had any voice. Here now as veterans who had risked
> their lives for the U.S. was the opportunity to do something
> about it.[15]

Further encouragement had come when doors of opportunity
opened during the war to Chicanos in industry, skilled trades,
and labor unions. The apparent opportunities proved to be short-
lived. Though a small, Mexican American middle class emerged
(by 1950 over seven percent of all employed Chicano males held
professional and other high white-collar positions as compared
to less than three percent in 1930), most discovered that new-
found opportunities were taken by Anglos returning from the
war. Others became victims of the downturn in business as the
nation shifted from a wartime to a peacetime economy. Still
others ran afoul of the antiunion sentiments fostered during the
Joseph McCarthy era of the 1950s. Many realized by the mid-
1950s that the struggle to win equal opportunity would remain
long and hard.

The pattern of institutional discrimination was still painfully
evident. Public facilities such as swimming pools commonly
excluded Mexicans, or limited use by them and other minorities until the day before the water was drained to avoid "con-
tamination." One such public pool in Corona openly shunned
Chicanos and other minorities by posting a sign which read
"For the White Race Only." Theaters in many communities
separated Mexicans by restricting them to "special seating sections," typically the balconies. Some business establishments

still had signs in their windows inviting "White Trade Only."
Chicanos also remained segregated residentially in barrios and
colonias, unable to move to better middle-class neighborhoods
partly because of economic reasons and partly because of real-
estate covenants which did not permit Mexicans and other non-
whites to rent or buy property in certain areas of a city. Communities in San Diego, Los Angeles, and Orange counties, for
example, had formal covenants which explicitly stated, "No
portion of the herein described property shall ever be sold,
conveyed, leased, occupied by, or rented to any person of any
Asiatic or African race . . . nor to any person of the Mexican
race."[16] Young Chicanos also suffered discrimination in public
education where segregation by school and classroom was widely
practiced. "All through Texas, New Mexico, Colorado, Arizona
and California, it is the same story," reported Stuart Barnes,
editor of *Speakers Magazine,* at the end of World War II. "Soldiers, returning veterans, heroes, come home to find that their
communities have turned traitor to the cause for which they
fought and bled. They have returned only to be 'put in their
place' — that place being, of course, on the bottom rung of the
Southwest's social and economic ladder."[17]

During the decade following the war, small groups of Chicanos contested various forms of discrimination. Mostly second-
generation Mexican Americans and members of the rising
middle class, they had benefited from the new opportunities
and persisted in their optimism for a brighter future. Some had
taken advantage of the G.I. Bill of Rights, which allowed
veterans access to higher education at little cost. For the first
time a significant number of Chicanos had entered the professional, managerial, proprietorial, clerical, and skilled occupations (see Table 3). "We acquired new ways in everyday doings,"
commented Raul Morín, and "new thoughts and dreams entered our minds. . . . We embarked on many unheard-of-for-us
projects and developed many ideas and new perspectives."[18]
These middle-class optimists spearheaded the struggle to advance civil rights and political representation for Chicanos.

Among the most vigorous of the reform organizations that
emerged during and after the war were the Unity Leagues and
the Community Service Organization (CSO) in California and
the American G.I. Forum in Texas. In the forefront of efforts in

California were the Unity Leagues established in Ontario, Po-
mona, and Chino, small towns about thirty miles east of Los
Angeles. Founded by Ignacio López, editor of the local Spanish-
language newspaper, *El Espectador,* the Unity Leagues challenged
discriminatory practices against Chicanos in public places and
in politics. Among their first targets was the public swimming
pool in nearby San Bernardino where Mexicans were refused
admittance. When López and a group of friends attempted to
enter the pool and were barred, they turned to the federal
courts. In *López v. Seccombe,* the district court in 1943 ruled that
San Bernardino had violated the civil rights of Mexican Americans and issued a permanent injunction forbidding the city to
bar Chicanos from the pool.

On another front, the Unity Leagues fought to assure Mexican Americans a political voice in local affairs. In Chino, where
Chicanos constituted nearly forty percent of the population, the
leagues led a voter registration drive that in 1946 resulted in an
ethnic bloc vote and the election of the first Mexican American,
Andrew Morales, to a city council seat. This success attracted
the interest of Fred Ross of the American Council on Race
Relations who helped establish Unity Leagues in Riverside and
San Bernardino counties and rallied Chicanos against school
segregation.[19]

The successes of the Unity Leagues inspired Chicanos in Los
Angeles to organize in 1947 the Community Service Organization as a vehicle to elect the first Mexican American to the Los
Angeles city council since 1881. This occurred in 1949 when
CSO, aided by Fred Ross, registered enough Mexican American
voters to put Edward Roybal in office. Although CSO continued
its voter registration drives—32,000 new Mexican American
voters were registered in east Los Angeles by 1950—it soon
shifted from endorsing specific candidates to fighting for civil
rights. Among its major triumphs were the "Bloody Christmas" and Hidalgo cases. On Christmas Eve 1951, Los Angeles
police officers arrested seven Chicano youths and, during their
interrogation at the Lincoln Heights station, severely beat
them. The beatings occurred while the officers were participating in a holiday drinking party at the station. CSO played a
major role in bringing about grand jury and FBI investigations
that resulted in the trial and conviction of five officers and the

suspension or dismissal of seventeen others. In 1956 CSO joined
with the American Civil Liberties Union to press the case of
thirteen-year-old David Hidalgo, a victim of an unprovoked
beating by two Los Angeles County deputy sheriffs. In a civil
suit, a jury found the two law enforcement officers guilty
of "police brutality," the first such verdict in Los Angeles history, and the judge ordered the sheriff's office to pay Hidalgo
damages. [20]

CSO chapters emerged in most California cities where Chicanos resided in sizable numbers, and they scored many civil
rights victories. In the early 1950s, however, those successes
became fewer as a result of the repressive Joseph McCarthy era
and the reluctant decision of CSO leaders to turn to less controversial activities such as providing mutual aid benefits to
members.

During the postwar years, Chicanos also banded into less
formal groups than CSO to correct local injustices. Some of
these ad hoc organizations produced significant results. For
example, in 1945 Chicano parents in Orange County set out to
desegregate the public schools. Several school districts in heavily populated Mexican areas segregated Chicanos into "all Mexican" schools. The parents took the Westminster School District
to court. School officials insisted that segregation of Mexican
students was not in violation of the Fifth and Fourteenth amend-
ments since it was done to provide special instruction required
by Spanish-speaking students and not because of their race or
nationality. In 1946 in *Méndez v. Westminster,* the Ninth Federal
District Court ruled against the Westminster School District
and three other Orange County school districts as well. Segregation of Mexicans, declared the court, violated the equal protection clauses of both the California and federal constitutions.
When the decision was later upheld by the U.S. Circuit Court
of Appeals, its impact was felt throughout the state. The decision prompted Governor Earl Warren to ask the legislature to
abolish the last statutes in California's Education Code that
permitted segregation. According to historian Charles Wollenberg, the Méndez case "ended nearly a century of *de jure* school
segregation in California and incorporated into the law the
integrationist and egalitarian morality that had developed during the 1930s and 1940s." [21]

Disappointment and Disillusion

THOUGH THE MÉNDEZ DECISION legally ended segregation in California's public schools, it did not affect de facto
segregation. As the Chicano population increased rapidly during the postwar decades and as the barrios expanded, the number of Mexican American children in ethnically isolated neighborhood schools rose dramatically. By 1970, there were more
Chicanos—nearly two-thirds of all school-age children—in segregated schools than in 1947 when the Méndez decision was
rendered.

Similar disappointments could be found in other areas. By
the early 1950s, most Chicano workers were still in unskilled
and semiskilled occupations. More than two-thirds of all Mexican American males and sixty-four percent of all females (see
Table 3) occupied the lowest rungs of the occupational ladder.
Though Chicano family median income in California increased
during the 1950s (from a level equivalent to seventy-five percent
of the Anglo family median income in 1949 to eighty percent
in 1959), this modest progress disappointed most second- and
third-generation native-born Mexican Americans who had hoped
for greater prosperity.[22]

Further disillusionment accompanied what became known
as "Operation Wetback." For several years after World War II
the Bracero Program could not accommodate the thousands of
additional workers in Mexico who wanted employment in the
U.S. Many crossed the border illegally, often encouraged by
southwestern growers who needed additional cheap labor because of the Korean War. When the war ended in 1953 and jobs
became scarce, the illegals found themselves unwelcomed and
publicly denounced as a major source of the nation's economic
problems. "Newspapers," notes historian Rodolfo Acuña, "re-
acted by calling for their exclusion and arousing anti-alien sentiments: undocumented workers were portrayed as dangerous,
malicious and subversive." These charges aroused the U.S.
Immigration and Naturalization Service, which responded by
rounding up undocumented Mexicans. Between 1953 and 1956
Chicano barrios experienced a wave of search-and-seizure tactics
reminiscent of the 1930s. Operation Wetback succeeded not

only in intimidating Chicano communities, but also in deporting over a million persons within three years. [23]

During World War II and the postwar years Chicanos won victories against discrimination and attained some measure of upward social mobility, but their struggle for an equitable "piece of the American pie" was obviously far from over. Though often disillusioned, they nonetheless prepared to renew the struggle during the 1960s.

CHAPTER SIX

Social Protest and Reform: The Rise of the Chicano Movement

TRADITIONAL AMERICAN VALUES and social institutions were sharply challenged in the 1960s and 1970s. The Vietnam War and the antiwar movement, the civil rights crusade, the urban race riots, the student protests on university and college campuses affected all Americans. These societal tensions led at first to civil rights, antipoverty, and other reforms, but by the mid-1970s a reaction to social legislation by state and federal governments was taking hold. People seemed resistant to examine what had happened to the nation and to consider alternatives. Reform and reaction thus characterized much of what occurred on the national scene during these two decades.

In California during this period, the disruption and soul-searching, social protest, racial discord, and fiscal conservatism reached dramatic levels. As depicted in the media, California often appeared to be the center of national agitation. Reference to student protests immediately conjured images of defiant young people surrounding buildings at the University of California, Berkeley; allusions to racial violence brought to mind the burning ruins of Watts; opposition to the Vietnam War became synonymous with the massive antiwar rallies in San Francisco; reaction to these protests was symbolized by the election of Governor Ronald Reagan and Senator S. I. Hayakawa, the passage of Proposition 13 and the resulting sharp reduction in government services, and the challenge to affirmative action in the U.S. Supreme Court decision of *Bakke v. University of California.*

Some of the dramatic protests of the 1960s and 1970s came from Mexican Americans seeking to draw the public's attention to their plight. In national magazines, stories of the "sleeping brown giant" raising its head emphasized that "mañana" had at last arrived for the state's largest and the country's second-largest minority. In California, their numbers alone meant that Chicanos could no longer be ignored. They were also no longer willing to accept wages, housing, education, and diet lower than the standards set for other Americans.

Catalysts of Change

THE 1960s were the crucible producing changes which unquestionably altered the character of Chicano society in California. The catalysts of change—demographic, ideological, and organizational—had roots dating from before World War II and, indeed, from the nineteenth century. Their significance in the late 1960s was that for the first time they coalesced and produced what became known as the Chicano movement.

Fundamental to the movement was the significant size of the Mexican population. Though their numbers in California had steadily multiplied during the decades of the twentieth century (even in the depression era the population had increased by nearly 50,000), the acceleration after World War II approached a population explosion. Between 1950 and 1960 the size of the state's Spanish-surnamed population doubled according to U.S. census enumerations (see Table 4). The actual increase was probably much greater since census counts have invariably missed large numbers of Hispanics, particularly undocumented Mexican immigrants. Enumerators have added to the confusion and

Table 4 : California Spanish Surname Population, 1930–1980
(identified variously by the U.S. Bureau of the Census)

Census Period (and U.S. census terminology)	Spanish Surname Population	Spanish Surnames as Percentage of Total Population
1980 (Spanish Origin)	4,543,770	19.2%
1970 (Spanish Origin)	2,369,292	11.9
1960 (Spanish Surname)	1,426,538	9.1
1950 (Spanish Surname)	758,400	7.2
1940 (Spanish Mother Tongue)	416,140	6.0
1930 (Mexican)	368,013	6.4

Source: U.S. Bureau of the Census population reports and *Subject Reports : Persons of Spanish Surname* (Spanish origin), 1960 and 1970 ; U.S. Bureau of the Census, Supplementary Report, PC80-SI-7, *Persons of Spanish Origin by State: 1980,* U.S. Government Printing Office, Washington, D.C., August 1982.

inaccurate counts by listing Mexicans and other Latin Americans under four different designations since 1930: Mexican in 1930, Spanish Mother Tongue in 1940, Spanish Surname in 1950 and 1960, Spanish Origin in 1970 and 1980. Again, from 1960 to 1970, the census registered a near doubling of the Spanish-origin population from approximately 750,000 to nearly a million and a half. With such numbers, Mexican Americans became aware of their potential clout in American politics and began intensifying their organizing efforts.

Groups such as the Community Service Organization and the Congress of Spanish Speaking Peoples had often advocated political action, but not until the creation in 1960 of the Mexican American Political Association (MAPA) did Chicanos initiate a statewide campaign to influence the policies of the two major political parties, especially the Democrats whom Chicanos had usually supported without receiving much in return. Capitalizing on widespread feelings of frustration, MAPA leaders organized as many as ninety local chapters throughout California which then engaged directly in electoral politics by sponsoring candidates, registering voters, informing Chicano communities about important issues, and lobbying for legislation that benefited the Mexican American constituency. Success came in the election of two Chicanos to the state assembly and the appointment of a few others to state judgeships. The successes, however, were limited and always short of expectations. Though keenly alert to political issues, MAPA also reflected characteristics associated with such traditional community organizations as mutualistas and other barrio self-help and defense groups. Beginning in the mid-1960s MAPA sponsored various ethnic-cultural celebrations and educational activities (a scholarship program for college-bound students, for example). In a sense, MAPA and its counterpart in Texas, the Political Association of Spanish Speaking People, became bridges between the older organizations and the highly politicized groups that emerged in the late 1960s.[1]

MAPA figured importantly in raising the political consciousness of Mexican Americans in California and in training a core of young professional political workers. The founding members of the organization, which included such veteran organizers as Bert Corona, Eduardo Quevedo, Sr., Edward Roybal, and Manuel Ruiz, Jr., gathered around them a host of new recruits whom they introduced to California politics. Many of these younger members later were appointed or elected to governmental positions on the local and state levels, while others helped establish such organizations as the National Council of La Raza (founded in 1968 as the Southwest Council of La Raza) which coordinated activities among Chicano community groups in the Southwest; the Mexican American Legal Defense and Education Fund or MALDEF (formed in 1968); and the Association of Mexican American Educators (an organization of teachers and administrators founded in 1965 to promote the education of Chicanos).

The Farm Workers' Movement

THE CATALYSTS PROMOTING Chicano political activity in the 1960s were primarily urban-based. This was not surprising given the overwhelming percentage of Mexican Americans living in California's cities by 1960 (eighty-five percent of the total Spanish-surnamed population). Ironically, though, perhaps the single most important development heightening the ethnic consciousness of Mexicans in California and dramatizing the plight of Chicanos to a national audience occurred in rural California: the farm workers' movement spearheaded by César Chávez. The national and international "Grape Boycott" declared in 1965 at Delano by the United Farm Workers (UFW) union brought widespread public attention to the exploitation and suffering of a most disadvantaged class of workers. But why did the UFW draw so much media attention and why did it generally succeed in its early labor-organizing efforts? After all, farm workers had tried to organize for decades without success. The answer lies partly in the UFW's ability to learn from mistakes made during earlier struggles by agricultural workers to gain control over their lives and partly in the ambiance of the mid-1960s that fostered support for the underdogs of American society.

Since the early twentieth century, but particularly since the labor strife of the 1930s in California agricultural fields, farm workers had sought to organize themselves. Their frustrated attempts continued into the 1940s when a forerunner of the UFW, the National Farm Labor Union (NFLU), became an AFL affiliate in 1947. In that same year NFLU Local 218 led a strike against the Di Giorgio Corporation in Arvin, a small town in the San Joaquin Valley. Two years later the strike ended when Local 218, lacking support from the parent union, succumbed to the pressure of a strong antiunion campaign. But the leaders of the strike, Ernesto Galarza and Henry Hasiwar, vowed to renew the struggle as soon as possible.

That opportunity came in 1952 when Local 218, still with only half-hearted backing from its parent union and with an almost nonexistent strike fund, called a strike against the Schenley Corporation, a major San Joaquin Valley producer of table grapes. Under heavy pressure from the growers, including their use of bracero workers to break the strike, union efforts once again collapsed. This second failure forced Galarza and his colleagues to reexamine their tactics. The bracero program in particular posed an insurmountable barrier to the establishment of a viable union. This barrier was not eliminated until 1964 when Congress terminated the program. By that time, however, the union (now renamed the National Agricultural Workers Union) had lost its charter and autonomy after being absorbed by an AFL trade union.[2]

Leadership in organizing agricultural workers then passed to
the recently chartered AFL-CIO Agricultural Workers Organizing Committee (AWOC). Led by Filipino workers, AWOC in
1965 struck against Delano grape growers. Shortly thereafter,
another union, the National Farm Workers Association (founded
in 1962 as the Farm Workers Association) headed by César
Chávez, joined the strike and took control. In many ways,
Chávez was the ideal leader for the new farm workers' movement. Born in Arizona, he had spent his adolescent years as a
migrant worker, moving with his parents with the seasons and
the harvests throughout the Southwest. In 1948 he settled with
his bride, Helen, in San Jose ,and there met Fred Ross of
the Community Service Organization who persuaded him to
join in the effort to organize local CSO chapters. His success in
that job earned Chávez a promotion in 1958 to general director
in California and Arizona. In 1962 he left CSO when it refused
to support his efforts to organize farm workers. He then moved
to Delano and together with his co-workers, principal among
them Dolores Huerta whom Chávez had met through CSO,
devoted his energies to building a union for people who labored
at back-breaking work for subsistence wages. Utilizing grass-
roots organizing strategies that he and Huerta had learned while
with CSO (the emphasis was on the "personal touch" and door-
to-door campaigning), the charismatic Chávez won over workers and attracted the attention of the American public. The
media presented Chávez, who from the beginning advocated
nonviolent tactics and staged dramatic marches to Sacramento
to publicize the struggles of the striking workers, as a Gandhi-
like leader of the noble, but oppressed toilers of the fields. His
appeals gained him financial support of the major labor unions
as well as the sympathy of the general public, and his efforts
became popularly known as "La Causa," the cause of social
justice for farm workers.

With such support, Chávez quickly won in 1966 the union's
first contract from the Schenley Corporation and immediately
sought a similar contract from the Di Giorgio farms, the neme-
sis of Galarza's union ten years earlier. A second victory for
Chávez, however, did not come so easily.

When negotiations with the major wine grape and table

grape growers failed, Chávez launched a boycott of markets everywhere and gained worldwide notoriety. The struggle between his United Farm Workers' Organizing Committee (the UFWA merged with the AFL-CIO's AWOC in 1967 to strengthen its position) and the grape growers grew more complex when the International Brotherhood of Teamsters, with the support of the grape growers, entered the dispute. The Teamsters battled Chávez over which union should organize field workers. The long grape strike and secondary boycott of national and international dimensions finally ended in 1970 when twenty-six growers, who faced financial losses and a bad public image, signed contracts with Chávez's union. The agreement guaranteed workers higher wages, union control of a hiring hall, and other concessions.

Though Chávez and his followers had won a strategic battle, the campaign was far from over and continued into the 1970s. The UFW (the UFWOC became a regular AFL-CIO union in 1972 and thus changed its name) staged strikes and encountered resistance as well as violence from lettuce growers in California and Arizona, from citrus growers in Florida, from the Teamsters, and from those California legislators in support of agribusiness. In 1975, the UFW achieved a major political victory when the state legislature, under the prodding of Governor Edmund G. "Jerry" Brown, Jr., passed a bill establishing the Agricultural Labor Relations Board. The ALRB's major responsibility was to assure farm workers secret elections so that they could choose freely which union, if any, they wished to represent them. The board was also to monitor the negotiations between workers and management. While the union has achieved some major victories, its future success cannot be taken for granted because every union victory has produced another round of conflict. Teamsters, growers, grower-supported politicians, and lobbyists seem bent on undermining the UFW. Increasing mechanization of agriculture and utilization of non-unionized workers, undocumented Mexican immigrants, and Southeast Asians have added to the problems of the UFW. Nonetheless, Chávez and his colleagues crusaded in a cause that is likely to endure and which as early as the 1960s had gained international attention.[3]

The Rise of the Chicano Movement

THE UNITED FARM WORKERS' struggles helped kindle the fire of Chicano resistance in the cities. To urban television viewers and newspaper and magazine readers, the UFW was engaging in a noble cause for a downtrodden people. By extension the farm workers' movement became a civil rights struggle for all disadvantaged Mexican Americans. In the cities, this struggle gave rise to the so-called "Chicano movement."

The Chicano movement included many elements: cultural renaissance, growing ethnic consciousness, proliferation of community and political organizations, social-reformist ideology, and civil rights advocacy. In some ways the earlier civil rights efforts of Chicanos dating from the 1930s combined with the black civil rights movement of the 1960s to provide the groundwork for the movement. The black reform efforts fostered sympathetic attitudes among white Americans toward all oppressed racial minorities. They also made Mexican Americans cognizant of how they and blacks faced similar problems and how change could come through mass mobilization and organization.

From their religious and national heritage the new urban Chicano leaders, like Chávez earlier, borrowed symbols of protest and ethnic solidarity: banners depicting the Virgin of Guadalupe, patron saint of Mexican Catholics; the Mexican national flag; and slogans and songs associated with Mexican revolutionary traditions and peasant heroes such as Emiliano Zapata. Other influences on the movement came from the "War on Poverty" program of Lyndon Johnson's administration. That program served as a kind of negative stimulus since it aroused the jealousy of many Chicano leaders who believed that federal agencies were too preoccupied with the welfare of blacks and had largely ignored Chicanos. Other issues galvanizing Chicanos included the maltreatment of undocumented Mexican immigrants by the Immigration and Naturalization Service, the high and disproportionate number of Chicano fatalities in the escalating Vietnam War, and the publications from governmental and educational agencies which provided data on the serious disadvantages faced by Mexican Americans. This information, when released in the 1960s, shattered perceptions of Mexican

American progress: high-school dropout rates often reached fifty percent; educational attainment, as measured by the median number of school years completed, lagged far behind Anglos (8.1 years as compared to 12.0 years); almost thirty-five percent of Spanish-surname households lived below the poverty level, a rate more than double that for Anglos; thirty percent of all dwellings occupied by Mexican Americans in the Southwest were classified as dilapidated as compared to only seven and a half percent of the buildings inhabited by Anglos; and Chicano unemployment was twice as high as that for Anglos. Such findings intensified Chicano demands for social reform.[4]

The Makeup of the "Movement"

THE CHICANO MOVEMENT meant different things to different people, both within and outside the Mexican American community. Clearly it was not, and still is not today, an easily defined or coordinated effort of all Chicanos. Indeed, it contains many disparate groups that sometimes quarreled: middle-class vs. working-class interests, youth vs. older generations, Californians vs. Texans, Marxists vs. non-Marxists, those who wished to work within existing structures vs. those who advocated alternative institutions. The Chicano movement in California also included people whose concerns ranged from the arts and humanities, community service, and religion to the rights of women and students. Some groups constituted mini-movements within the larger Chicano movement.[5]

Among the most creative individuals of the 1960s and 1970s were Chicano artists, poets, writers, playwrights, and actors. Mostly young people of the second generation, their work reflected the cultural and political message of the Chicano activists. Especially dramatic contributions were the vivid murals that decorated otherwise drab barrio walls and buildings (e.g., the Estrada Court murals of east Los Angeles and the murals in Chicano Park in San Diego), theater performances (e.g., the Teatro Campesino and the plays directed by Luis Valdez, most notably *Zoot Suit*), political posters (e.g., those by Rupert García and Malaquías Montoya), and many published works of poetry and fiction. These imaginative people worked as individuals and in such groups as La Galería de la Raza in San Francisco, Mujeres Muralistas (women muralists), and the Rebel Chicano Art Front (also known as the Royal Chicano Air Force) founded in 1972 in Sacramento by a group of graphic artists. Many drew upon the past for their techniques and ideas. For example, the muralists borrowed heavily from the great Mexican artists Diego Rivera, José Orozco, and David Siquieros, while the teatro performers followed an art form long practiced among Mexicans in the U.S. But they also took their inspiration from more recent events, especially the cultural renaissance accompanying the political resurgence of the 1960s and 1970s.[6]

Perhaps the most widespread phenomenon of the Chicano movement was the proliferation of community service organizations. They ran the gamut from federally financed employment and drug rehabilitation programs to so-called community development corporations (CDCs). Many assumed multiple roles and thus overlapped in purpose, while others were organized along narrow political or ideological lines. Some were funded privately or through federal, state, or local agencies, while others obtained support from a variety of sources. Most groups, regardless of purpose or source of funding, served a relatively small, well-defined constituency.

The community service groups included mental health centers like the Centro de Salud Mental in Oakland, medical care facilities like the East Los Angeles Free Clinic, job-training programs like the Chicana Service Action Center in Los Angeles, drug rehabilitation programs, legal aid clinics, "pinto" (ex-convict) programs, and community corporations like The East Los Angeles Community Union, or TELACU, which was originally an antipoverty group that became a corporation devoted to the economic development of Chicano-owned or managed businesses. Community service organizations generally had their origins in the demands of barrio residents who joined with a small corps of Chicano and Anglo middle-class professionals to devise solutions to problems. Since these service groups were usually dependent on public funding, most of it coming from Lyndon Johnson's "War on Poverty" programs, their capacity to operate successfully was greatly affected by periods of economic recession and political-fiscal conservatism.

Nonetheless, they provided critically needed services in the barrio and served as a training arena for Chicanos in health care and social services as well as in the government bureaucracies.[7]

Other prominent organizations of the late 1960s and 1970s were those dedicated to political action and public policy. Noteworthy were the Mexican American Legal Defense and Education Fund (MALDEF) and the Southwest Council of La Raza (renamed the National Council of La Raza), both of which remain active. Though the two groups were founded by Chicano professionals (primarily attorneys, educators, and labor union officials), they differed in their philosophies and methods. MALDEF, headquartered in San Francisco and supported initially by the Ford Foundation, focused on defending the legal, educational, and civil rights of Chicanos. Since its founding in 1968, but especially under the leadership of Vilma Martínez in the 1970s, MALDEF fought numerous court battles over school desegregation, employment discrimination, and bilingual education. In recent years it has taken on issues ranging from the educational rights of children of undocumented immigrants to the under-enumeration of Hispanics by the U.S. Census Bureau. With regional offices throughout the country, MALDEF also helped launch the careers of a new generation of Chicano attorneys.

The National Council of La Raza, like MALDEF, also emerged in the late 1960s, especially as a result of the efforts of Chicano labor and community organizers, including Bert Corona and Ernesto Galarza. It too received support from the Ford Foundation, but its goal was to become an umbrella organization coordinating the activities of local community groups in California and the Southwest. At first, it followed MALDEF's example and ventured into the area of public policy by examining the delivery of social services and voting patterns among Los Angeles Chicanos. By the early 1970s, however, the Council had changed its focus because of demands made by the Ford Foundation and because of the changing composition of its leadership. It then concentrated on establishing specific development programs in barrios, such as a community-based corporation to promote better housing. When those programs failed because of administrative inexperience and insufficient funds, the Council transformed itself into a national lobby for Hispanics.[8]

Three other organizations emerged at roughly the same time as the Council and MALDEF, but differed greatly from them in ideology and programs. La Raza Unida Party (LRUP) first appeared in 1970 when some Chicano students in several rural, predominantly Mexican, towns in south Texas contested the domination of local politics by Anglo Democrats and Republicans. Under the leadership of José Angel Gutiérrez, these young activists established their own political party, nominated candidates, and won important positions on school boards and city councils and a few mayoralty races. Encouraged by their initial success, they organized parties in other southwestern states, including California. LRUP candidates never won the firm support of Chicanos in California cities as they had in Texas towns, but the party tallied some modest successes in the San Bernardino area where it helped elect two Chicanos to the Cucamonga school board and, together with other political groups, succeeded in electing the first Chicano to the city council of Ontario. These small victories revealed the potential power of the Chicano vote and reflected a growing political consciousness among young Chicanos frustrated by the inattention of the two major political parties.[9]

The National Chicano Moratorium, unlike LRUP, was not a political party, but rather a coalition of groups opposed to the Vietnam War and the disproportionate numbers of Chicano battle fatalities. Chicano casualties between 1961 and 1967, according to Professor Ralph Guzmán, accounted for about nineteen percent of all servicemen from the Southwest killed in action. The National Chicano Moratorium Committee, initially sponsored by the Brown Berets, a quasi-military group of young radicals, held protest marches in Los Angeles in late 1969 and again in 1970, where the largest drew between twenty and thirty thousand people from across the nation. The latter demonstration culminated on August 29 in a gathering in Laguna Park where the crowd listened to music and speeches. Those present included men and women, the young and the elderly, non-Chicanos as well as Chicanos, many carrying banners and all excited by the occasion. During mid-afternoon an incident involving shoplifting at a nearby liquor store prompted the large, ready force of police to converge on the store. The overreaction by police aroused the anger of Chicanos nearby. Within minutes the incident turned into an assault by riot police, not only on those at the liquor store, but also on the people in the park. The bewildered crowd scattered for safety. Tear-gassings, clubbings, rock and bottle throwing, stampedes and looting led to major property losses in the nearby business district. Many injuries and some deaths occurred, the most controversial being the slaying by police of Rubén Salazar, a well-known reporter for the *Los Angeles Times* and popular personality on the local Spanish-language television station. The events of August 29 produced bitterness in Chicano communities across the nation and sparked many heretofore complacent people into joining in the struggle for civil rights. [10]

Among those on the National Chicano Moratorium Committee were representatives from CASA (Centro de Acción Social Autónoma–Hermandad General de Trabajadores, or Center for Autonomous Social Action–General Brotherhood of Workers). Founded in 1968, it focused primarily on single, critical issues, especially those involving undocumentd Mexican workers. Its cofounders were Soledad "Chole" Alatorre, a union organizer, and Bert Corona, a member of the Congreso during the 1930s,

"March of Resistance" sponsored by CASA, East Los Angeles, 1975. (*Reproduced from the records of the CASA Collection {Centro de Acción Social Autónoma} ms. 325, Department of Special Collections, Stanford University Libraries*)

a leader in the International Longshoremen's Union during the 1940s, and a cofounder of MAPA. They drew on their rich experience to provide legal defense and social services to Mexican immigrants and to educate the public about the complexities of U.S. immigration policy. The value of such an organization was immediately apparent and local CASA chapters sprang up in other American cities which had sizable populations of undocumented Mexican workers.

In the mid-1970s Corona, Alatorre, and other CASA leaders were challenged by younger members of the group, many of whom were Marxists determined to change the direction of the organization. As the founding leaders resigned, the newcomers launched a "Marxist-Leninist revolutionary" program dedicated to mobilizing and politicizing Chicano and undocumented workers. They published a newspaper, *Sin Fronteras* (Without Borders), as a vehicle for spreading their ideas and winning recruits. Internal organizational problems — ideological, financial, and otherwise — combined with surveillance and infiltration by the FBI and Los Angeles police to thwart CASA's goal of emerging at the forefront of the Chicano movement. By the late 1970s CASA's membership was moving to other organizations. [11]

The CASA experience resembled that of many Chicano organizations of the 1960s and 1970s, including those established by students. Mexican American organizations on California college campuses began to emerge as small numbers of Chicano students gained admittance in the late 1960s. Though thousands of Mexican Americans used the G.I. Bill of Rights after World War II to pursue higher education, the large majority attended two-year community colleges. Chicano students remained grossly underrepresented in the state's principal colleges and universities during most of the 1960s. In 1965, for example, UCLA had fewer than a hundred students out of a total enrollment of over twenty-five thousand, while only seven Chicanos were enrolled at California State University, Northridge. Within three years, federal grant and loan programs (such as the Educational Opportunity Program and National Defense and Education Loans Program), together with special admission programs for minority students, enabled thousands of Chicanos to attend colleges throughout the state. These students in turn rallied around such campus issues as the underrepresentation of

Mexican American students and the growing antiwar movement. In addition, the farm workers' struggles provided ethnic and ideological ammunition to stir student feelings. By the late 1960s, Chicano students followed many banners on various campuses: the Mexican American Student Association (MASA) at East Los Angeles Community College, United Mexican American Students (UMAS) at Loyola University and UCLA, and the Mexican American Student Confederation (MASC), an umbrella organization encompassing several groups in the San Francisco Bay area. These organizations had counterparts almost everywhere in the Southwest where parallel groups of black students formed. [12]

The Chicano student movement in California received major stimulus from protests in the spring of 1968. These outbursts took place on high school rather than college campuses, but dealt with issues of broad concern. The principal instigator was Saul Castro, a Los Angeles teacher made angry by what he observed in the predominantly Chicano high schools of east Los Angeles. To draw attention to classroom conditions, Castro publicly criticized the overcrowded rooms, the inadequate number of Chicano teachers and administrators, the curriculum which ignored the contributions of Chicanos, and the lack of programs to reduce the high dropout rates. Supported by local community groups and Chicano students from nearby colleges, Castro led nearly ten thousand students in the five local east Los Angeles high schools in a boycott of their classes. These so-called "blow-outs" attracted wide media attention when police attempts to disperse the demonstrators resulted in violence. Besides spotlighting the inequalities in the schools and paving the way for some educational reforms, the student walkouts inspired Chicanos in high schools and colleges in California and elsewhere to organize on behalf of other causes. [13]

In an effort to unite the many campus groups, student leaders in 1969 called a statewide conference in Santa Barbara and established the Movimiento Estudiantil Chicano de Aztlán or MECHA (Chicano Student Movement of Aztlán). They set forth their goals in a document known as the Plan de Santa Bárbara. According to historian Juan Gómez-Quiñones, it called for "a unified common philosophy, strategy and curriculum for Chicano Studies programs and student organizations in California

March down Brooklyn Avenue in east Los Angeles sponsored by Centro de Acción Social Autónoma (CASA) to demonstrate support for the rights of undocumented workers, circa 1973. (*Reproduced through the courtesy of the Department of Special Collections, Stanford University {CASA Manuscript Collection}.*)

as a whole and ultimately nationally." Almost immediately, however, students began quarreling among themselves over tactics and ideology. Despite their often heated disagreements, they succeeded in helping to establish Chicano studies programs on most California college campuses, in pressuring faculty and administrators into taking steps to increase the number of Chicano students and professors, and in enriching the cultural diversity of institutions of higher learning. [14]

Among those making the most significant contributions to the Chicano movement were women. Chicanas did not suddenly assert themselves in the 1960s, for earlier such women as Luisa Moreno, Josephine Fierro de Bright, Dolores Huerta, and Soledad Alatorre had held prominent leadership positions. Sometimes they worked separately from their male counterparts, while on other occasions they campaigned alongside men. In many cases, they were the prime movers of such organizing efforts as the Spanish Speaking People's Congress, the UFW, CASA, and MALDEF.

Still, only a small minority of Chicanas played major roles before the 1960s when civil rights and feminist movements raised women's consciousness about themselves and their status in society. They at first questioned the Chicano movement itself, a movement that espoused justice and equality while relegating most women to inferior positions. They demanded that men reassess their views about the ability of women to make major contributions, especially as leaders. If women were to be integral members of the community, they had to be seen as something more than wives, mothers, and daughters. They demanded an end to the inequality they had faced both in and out of Chicano society because of their gender, ethnicity, and class.

The Chicana movement produced dynamic state and national leaders. By the early 1970s, Vilma Martínez had emerged as president of MALDEF and Dolores Huerta was a driving force and vice president in the UFW. Other women emerged into prominence as the result of their efforts in such groups as the Los Angeles–based Comisión Femenil Mexicana Nacional, formed in 1970 to train Chicanas for leadership roles, and the Chicana Service Action Center, established by long-time organizer Francisca Flores to help working-class women hone their occupational skills. Other organizations, ranging from homes for battered wives to campus support groups, materialized after 1970 as Chicanas organized to help themselves and to advance Mexican Americans everywhere.[15]

Among those institutions long sacred to both women and men and also resistant to change is the Roman Catholic church. In Mexico and the U.S. the church is the center of the religious lives of a majority of Mexicans and has been since the days of Spanish colonization. Catholicism indelibly stamps many of the customs, folkways, and compadrazgo relationships on Mexican parishioners. The church is usually omnipresent throughout an individual's life cycle: baptism soon after birth, first communion during early childhood, confirmation during adolescence, marriage during young adulthood, and the last rites at death. Though Chicanos, like most Catholics, vary in their degree of religiosity, most have remained close to the church. Only recently have some openly criticized church policies or begun in significant numbers to marry outside the church, or not to marry at all.

Though the Catholic parishes in barrio neighborhoods have been concerned about the general welfare of their members, many Chicanos believed that concern to be less than it should be. After all, they claimed, for centuries Mexicans faithfully gave of themselves on behalf of the church and the church should now provide more economic aid and support their efforts to obtain social justice. In 1969 some Los Angeles Chicanos, particularly women, established Católicos por La Raza in order to dramatize the church's insensitivity. During the same year others decried the failure of the clergy to speak out on behalf of the farm workers, a failure that seemed all the more glaring because Protestant clergy were demonstrating more concern than Catholic priests. The church hierarchy only modestly accommodated to the needs of Chicano Catholics, mostly in the form of Spanish-language services and utilization of Chicano priests. Hispanic bishops had been appointed in dioceses throughout the Southwest, but few held positions of power. Some Chicano clergy have joined ranks and formed a group called PADRES (Padres Asociados por Derechos Religiosas, Educativos y Sociales, or Associated Priests for Religious, Educational, and Social Rights) to advocate for change within the church and for additional Chicano priests. At least some of the hierarchy have also responded with support for Chicano struggles. The Bishops' Committee on Farm Labor supported the UFW grape strike, while the United Neighborhood Organizations, a group of Catholic and Protestant church leaders in Los Angeles, agitated for economic opportunities for their Chicano churchgoers.[16]

The Movement's Legacy

THE CHICANO MOVEMENT, that aggregation of many different ideologies, philosophies, and organizational strategies, was the natural by-product of an era that witnessed heightened ethnic consciousness not only of Mexican Americans but also of other disadvantaged groups. The intensity of the 1960s and 1970s has waned in the 1980s, but the movement produced advances that have been woven into the fabric of California life. Among the principal legacies is the positive self-identity that the movement fostered among Mexican Americans. Such ethnic pride helped propel the demands for socioeconomic and political reform. Though the movement did not bring the sweeping changes which some people had envisioned, it succeeded in educating the general public about the largest group of Hispanics. It also significantly improved avenues of advancement in higher education, employment, and business, and, in addition, brought about major civil rights gains. As historian Carlos Cortés has aptly noted:

> The Chicano movement is not the whole story of contemporary Mexican Americans, nor has it won the unanimous support of the group. Some question whether militant ethnic solidarity is the best tactic for advancement, but the movement has been a galvanizing force for change, whatever its ultimate effects prove to be.[17]

Put another way, the Chicano movement reflected the aspirations and frustrations of the nation's second-largest minority and became a vehicle for advancing the cause of social justice.

Mexican Americans in the 1980s

S OME MEXICAN AMERICANS speak only English and identify only with the U.S., while others speak mostly Spanish
and consider themselves "Mexicano" rather than Mexican American or Chicano. The younger generation of the middle class
may have their sights on university educations, while the
schooling expectations of Chicano working-class youth may end
during high school as dropouts. Some Mexican Americans live
in comfortable suburban homes, while others inhabit dilapidated dwellings in the large barrios. Some may claim roots two
hundred years old in the state, while others may be undocumented immigrants who crossed the border yesterday. These
contrasts apply to Americans of Mexican descent in California,
a dramatically expanding, diverse population whose visibility
will surely increase as the century comes to a close. Though
individual diversity exists, the status of most Mexican Americans has been shaped largely by common historical experiences.
They also will share a common future. As demographic change in
the Mexican population continues, two principal developments
—educational attainment and occupational advancement—will
greatly influence the direction of Mexican American society
in the 1990s and beyond. A difficult challenge confronts all

Californians: Will the growing Mexican American population successfully integrate into society or will the debilitating socio-economic inequalities experienced by past generations continue into the next century?

Demographic Growth and Distribution

CALIFORNIA'S MEXICAN POPULATION experienced significant demographic change during the 1970s and early 1980s. The 1980 census recorded a sharp rise in the number of Mexican Americans and Mexican immigrants. Remarkably, the state's Hispanic or Spanish-origin population nearly doubled between 1970 and 1980, according to U.S. census figures. Today, Hispanics number over 4.5 million—over twenty percent of the state's total population—constituting nearly a third of all Latinos in the nation. The great majority of these people, over eighty percent, are of Mexican origin. Almost forty-two percent of all Mexicans in the U.S. live in California.[1]

Since 1970, the growth in the Mexican-origin population has been concentrated in the southern counties. Between 1970 and 1980, for example, the increase of the Spanish-origin population in Los Angeles, Orange, and San Diego counties was approximately sixty, seventy-nine, and fifty-eight percent respectively. Only Santa Clara County, located in the San Francisco Bay area, exhibited an increase in the number of Mexicans comparable to its counterparts in the south. In 1980, Los Angeles County remained the center of the Mexican American and immigrant population. Over two million Spanish-origin people live within the county's boundaries, about twenty-eight percent of the county's total population (see map). As many as half of all Mexicans in the state reside in Los Angeles County (see Table 5). Three other counties, Santa Clara, Orange, and San Diego, also have large Hispanic communities numbering between 225,000 and 286,000. Five other counties have Mexican populations exceeding 100,000. The Mexican population in California is certain to grow rapidly due to a high birth rate, a young median

Table 5 : Rank Order of the Fifteen Counties with Largest
Hispanic Population, State of California, 1980

Rank	County	Total Population	Hispanic Population	Hispanics as Percentage of Total
—	STATE	23,668,562	4,543,770	19.2%
1	Los Angeles	7,477,657	2,065,727	27.6
2	Orange	1,931,570	286,331	14.8
3	San Diego	1,861,846	275,176	14.8
4	Santa Clara	1,295,071	226,611	17.5
5	San Bernardino	893,157	165,295	18.5
6	Fresno	515,013	150,820	29.3
7	Alameda	1,105,379	129,962	11.8
8	Riverside	663,923	124,496	18.7
9	Ventura	529,899	113,241	21.4
10	Kern	403,089	87,025	21.6
11	San Francisco	678,974	83,373	12.3
12	Monterey	290,444	75,129	25.9
13	Sacramento	783,381	74,139	9.5
14	San Mateo	588,164	73,362	12.5
15	Tulare	245,751	73,296	29.8
	TOTAL	19,253,318	4,003,983	20.8
	Percentage of Statewide Population	81.4%	88.1%	

Source : Compiled from 1980 Census of Population and Housing, U.S. Bureau of
the Census.

age, and immigration from Mexico. Mexican women in their
prime childbearing ages (twenty through twenty-nine) are estimated to have on the average 169 births per thousand women
per year compared to 120 births for the total population. In
1980, Hispanics in general, and Mexican Americans in particular, were one of the youngest populations in the nation, with a
median age of twenty-three years; by comparison, the median
age for non-Hispanic whites is thirty-two years. When com-
paring Hispanics and non-Hispanics, the youngest and oldest
age groups reveal in even sharper relief the relative youthfulness
of the group: thirty-five percent of all Hispanics, but only
twenty-one percent of non-Hispanic whites, are under fourteen

years old, while the age group sixty-five years and older accounts for only four and a half percent of Hispanics and twelve percent of non-Hispanic whites.[2]

Immigration from Mexico

P OPULATION PROJECTIONS for Hispanics up to the year
2000 estimate that natural increase will account for approximately sixty-two percent of the group's net growth. The other major source of increase has been, and will continue to be, immigration from Mexico.[3] This phenomenon is more than a century old, but in the 1900s immigration must be viewed in the context of international labor migration and the political economy of the U.S. and Mexico as well as within the longer history of people moving back and forth across the border. The hundreds of thousands who entered the U.S. during the past twenty years are part of a fourth cycle of immigration from Mexico during the current century. The most recent flow of migrants began in the 1960s (after the termination of the Bracero Program, Public Law 78, in 1964), but their full impact was not felt until the 1970s and 1980s. Mexican undocumented immigrants have been arriving in California—the largest percentage of Mexican immigrants in the U.S. reside in the state— in unprecedented numbers for over a decade. The exact numbers are impossible to come by, but scholarly estimates range from a high of about 3 million to a low of approximately 500,000; the actual number, no doubt, lies somewhere between these extremes.[4]

According to a recent study of the 1980 census, nearly 600,000 undocumented Mexican immigrants and another 250,-000 Mexican legal immigrants live in California (this same study estimated that the 1980 census undercounted between 100,000 and 150,000 "illegal" immigrants from Mexico in southern California). The great majority of the state's recent Mexican immigrants live in the southern counties, especially in Los Angeles County where over fifty percent are estimated to reside. Only about twenty-five percent of the post-1970 Mexican immigrants have made their way to the northern counties.[5]

Mexican immigrants, both legal and undocumented, have created readily visible as well as less perceptible changes in California society. In the most dramatic instances, immigrants have contributed to enormous demographic changes affecting the existing Mexican American communities. From the border cities like San Ysidro, to the fast-growing urban centers like San Diego and San Jose with their large metropolitan populations, to the Los Angeles metropolis, immigration has increased the concentration of people in, and expanded the boundaries of, barrios throughout California. Immigrants have reinforced the use of the Spanish language in barrios in east Los Angeles where, for example, one can walk along the main business thoroughfares and hear Spanish spoken almost exclusively. Businesses catering to the new arrivals are apparent everywhere in barrios: new small grocery stores selling regional Mexican foods, entertainment establishments providing dancing, music, and other forms of recreation—everything from a "Discoteca Michoacana" dance hall to a "Jalisco" restaurant. Among the most important developments arising from recent immigration from Mexico is the growth of a new generation of native-born children with expectations and horizons as Mexican Americans, a generation much different from its immigrant parents. In many ways, the process of immigration and adjustment to life in the U.S. for this most recent group of immigrants and their children is being reenacted for the fourth time in California in this century. Though the various cycles of Mexican immigration to California are similar, society has changed greatly over time, consequently making the experiences of each wave of Mexican immigrants somewhat different.

Immigrants will continue to arrive in large numbers as long as Mexico is beset with a low standard of living, rampant inflation, devaluation of the peso, and high unemployment. Neither increased border surveillance nor changes in U.S. immigration law will stem the tide of large-scale migration until the economic problems of Mexico are brought under control. As long as large numbers of people cannot support themselves or their families in the Mexican economy, they will seek employment in the U.S. as a means to stave off the starvation and destitution they face in their homeland.

Education

O NE OF THE BIG CHALLENGES facing California over the
next twenty years will be the education of Mexican immigrant and Mexican American children. The schools perhaps
more than any single institution in the state are now experiencing the impact of the Mexican population explosion. In
1981, every fourth pupil in state public schools, grades K
through 12, was Hispanic. In the Los Angeles Unified School
District, twenty-nine percent of all students were Hispanic in
1979, but by 1981 their percentage had increased to thirty-
nine. Today, in Los Angeles Unified, the nation's second-largest
district, nearly every other student is Hispanic. The rapid
growth rate of Hispanic youngsters in Los Angeles schools not
only reflects a high birth rate and immigration from Mexico,
but also the steady decline of Anglo students who leave public
education for private schools.[6]

Mexican American students are especially concentrated in
the primary schools in California where they constitute over
thirty-four percent of all kindergartners and twenty-four percent of all sixth graders. The percentages of Hispanics enrolled
in the higher grades, however, rapidly fall, especially in the
high schools. Hispanics make up twenty-two percent of all
tenth graders, but form only seventeen percent of all seniors. In
California and in other states where Mexican Americans are a
large minority, school failure measured by dropout rates is ex-
tremely high. Statistics for the years 1974–1978 show that
nearly half of all Chicano students left high school before
graduation.[7]

Whatever indicator is used to assess the performance of Mexican Americans in the public schools — high school graduates,
reading scores, scholastic aptitude test scores, dropout rates —
the results show that a schooling gap still exists between Chicanos and Anglos, a gap that increases significantly beginning
in secondary schools and on through higher education. Almost
a third of all Hispanic adults in California have only an eighth-
grade education. Less than twenty percent of all California Hispanics attend colleges and universities in contrast to about forty-
three percent of all non-Hispanics who attain some level of
higher education.[8]

Some progress has been made: twenty years ago few Chicanos could be found on any California college campus. By 1980, however, the California state universities, the University of California campuses, and private institutions of higher education in the state had Chicano enrollments comprising nine, six, and eight percent of their student bodies respectively. A majority of the Mexican Americans in higher education are enrolled in California community colleges.[9]

As public school and higher education resources grow smaller and the Chicano and other minority school populations increase, the challenge for California's institutions of learning will be whether they can educate productive citizens or whether they will fail and turn out individuals who are unable to contribute to the welfare of themselves, their ethnic communities, or society at large. Education has long served as one of the principal institutions promoting individual and group upward mobility in American society. The historical record shows that the public schools have been important forces in the socioeconomic progress of Chicanos, but not to the same degree they have served other ethnic and immigrant groups in the U.S. The education of the current generation of Mexican American students will largely determine their status in the next century.

Employment

THE SLIGHT GAIN made by Chicanos in education during the 1960s and 1970s parallels the modest improvements in occupation (see Table 3). Males have made slow but steady occupational gains in high white-collar (professional and managerial), low white-collar (clerical and sales), skilled (craftsmen and foremen), and semiskilled or low blue-collar jobs. During the same years, the percentage of unskilled workers (laborers and farm workers) has steadily declined. Women have also improved their occupational status. The percentage of female clerical workers has risen while the percentage of semiskilled factory workers (operatives) declined. State and federally funded employment development programs focusing on job training and placement have contributed to Chicanos' occupational progress over the past fifteen years.

A raid by agents of the Immigration and Naturalization Service on a downtown Los Angeles garment factory and apprehension of Mexican workers sometime during the 1970s. (*Reproduced from the records of the* CASA *Collection {Centro de Acción Social Autónoma} ms. 325, Department of Special Collections, Stanford University Libraries*)

The fact remains, however, that occupational mobility for Chicanos has been painfully slow and frustrating. The historical disparities between the employment status of Hispanics and Anglos continues. According to a state survey conducted in 1978, fifty-six percent of the total employed population in California worked in higher status white-collar positions compared to thirty percent for Hispanics. Blue-collar jobs were held by forty-nine percent of all Hispanic workers, but only twenty-nine percent for all other workers. Hispanics routinely have a higher jobless rate than do most Anglo workers. In 1979, for example, Hispanics in California consistently maintained an unemployment rate 2.3 percentage points above that of non-Hispanics (8.5 percent compared to 6.2 percent).[10]

A report issued in 1981 by the California Health and Welfare Agency and the Employment Development Department poignantly characterized the labor-market conditions of Hispanic workers:

The available data suggests that Hispanics as a group are not successfully employed in California's labor markets. Many factors could be contributing to their relatively poor position in the job market; specifying definite causes and effects is difficult given the quality of the existing data. There is little doubt, however, that the relatively low educational attainment of Hispanics has had a negative impact on Hispanic employment. In addition, patterns of employment discrimination still persist, despite federal guarantees of equal opportunity. The cycle of poverty in which a disproportionate number of Hispanic families find themselves tends to be self-perpetuating; poor nutrition and health conditions, crime, violence, and a general negative atmosphere do not create expectations of success; expectations which are taken for granted in the majority of middle-class and non-minority households.[11]

Indeed, the poor employment conditions of Hispanics are merely one dimension of the cycle perpetuating the low socioeconomic status they occupy in California. Low educational attainment means low occupational attainment. Poor-paying jobs translate into a struggle between financial subsistence and poverty (in 1970, for example, Chicano family income was twenty-seven percent below that for Anglo families, and in 1978 Hispanic average household income was twenty-four percent below non-Hispanics). Poverty forces people to be preoccupied with daily survival rather than setting goals that may promote long-term mobility. Though a majority of Mexican Americans have not escaped this cycle of low socioeconomic status, many have broken free of it, indicating that upward mobility is possible if doors of opportunity are opened to larger numbers of young people.

"The Decade of the Hispanic"

JOBS AND EDUCATION, today as in the past, are the two issues of primary concern for Chicanos. Upward occupational mobility and higher education are keys to a better standard of living in American society. In recent years, national magazines and newspapers have presented the theme of Hispanic American progress, portraying the 1980s as the "Decade of the Hispanic" and suggesting that Chicanos, Puerto Ricans, Cubans, Central and South Americans will soon experience upward social mobility as have countless other immigrants in the U.S.[12]

Yes, Chicanos and other Hispanics are growing more aware of themselves as a force in society, and society at large is growing more aware of them. To depict Chicanos in California as a group steadily moving upward into the American mainstream, however, is to distort historical and contemporary reality. Clearly, progress has been achieved by thousands of Chicanos, but one should not think that Mexican Americans are necessarily destined to follow the paths of such European immigrants in the U.S. as the Germans, Irish, Italians, Poles, or other nationalities. The history of conflict, socioeconomic and political discrimination, and negative racial attitudes separates Chicanos from past immigrant groups. History seems to have set Chicanos' trajectory in American society on a different course, certainly one more analogous to most blacks, Indians, and some Asians than to white Europeans. Perhaps by the twenty-first century the strong currents in history that have weighed the group down for so long will change in a positive direction as Chicanos strive to create a significant and meaningful life for themselves in California society.

NOTES

CHAPTER ONE

1. The works of Hubert Howe Bancroft still provide the best detailed data for the colonial period; see especially his *History of California* (7 vols., San Francisco: A. L. Bancroft, 1884–1890).

2. Carey McWilliams, *North from Mexico: The Spanish-Speaking People of the United States* (1948; New York: Greenwood Press, 1968), 35–47; see also Leonard Pitt, *The Decline of the Californios: A Social History of the Spanish-Speaking Californians, 1846–1890* (Berkeley and Los Angeles: University of California Press, 1966), 84–93.

3. See Hubert H. Bancroft, *California Pastoral, 1769–1848* (San Francisco: The History Co., 1888), and Irving B. Richman, *California under Spain and Mexico* (Boston: Houghton Mifflin, 1911). Population figures for non-Indians during the colonial period vary somewhat, but most numbers approximate those cited in the text; see, for example, David Hornbeck, *California Patterns: A Geographical and Historical Atlas* (Palo Alto, Calif.: Mayfield, 1983), 50–51; John F. Bannon, *The Spanish Borderlands Frontier, 1513–1821* (New York: Holt, Rinehart & Winston, 1970), 224; David J. Weber, *The Mexican Frontier, 1821–1846* (Albuquerque: University of New Mexico Press, 1982), 6.

4. For the effects of secularization of the missions, see Pitt, *Decline of the Californios,* 7–8; Robert G. Cleland, *The Cattle on a Thousand Hills* (San Marino, Calif.: Huntington Library, 1951), 19–20; and Bancroft, *History of California,* III, 649–651; Weber, *Mexican Frontier,* 64–67, 208.

5. Pitt, *Decline of the Californios,* 10.

6. Richard Griswold del Castillo, *The Los Angeles Barrio, 1850–1890* (Berkeley and Los Angeles: University of California Press, 1979), 13–21; Albert Camarillo, *Chicanos in a Changing Society: From Mexican Pueblos to American Barrios in Santa Barbara and Southern California, 1846–1930* (Cambridge: Harvard University Press, 1979),

8–13, 101–107; Weber, *Mexican Frontier,* 228–229; Hornbeck, *California Patterns,* 49–51, 58–59; Antonia I. Castañeda, "Cholas, Californianas, and Chicanas: Mexican Women in Northern California, 1785–1870" (Ph.D. dissertation, Stanford University, in progress). For a discussion of the political changes brought about by republicanism, see Weber, *Mexican Frontier,* 15–42.

7. *Ibid.,* 215–217; Antonio I. Castañeda, "The Political Economy of Nineteenth-Century Stereotypes of Californianas," paper presented at the Pacific Coast Branch, American Historical Association (San Francisco, August 1982); Griswold del Castillo, *Los Angeles Barrio,* 14.

8. For examples of various stereotypes, see Richard Henry Dana, *Two Years Before the Mast* (1846; New York: Bantam Books, 1959); Alfred Robinson, *Life in California* (1846; Santa Barbara, Calif.: Peregrine Press, 1970); Thomas Jefferson Farham, *Travels in California and Scenes in the Pacific* (1844; Oakland, Calif.: Biobooks reprint, 1947). For analyses of these and other stereotypes, see Cecil Robinson, *Mexico and the Hispanic Southwest in American Literature* (Tucson: University of Arizona Press, 1977), 41–43; Castañeda, "Political Economy of Stereotypes"; David Langum, "California Women and the Image of Virtue," *Southern California Quarterly,* LIX (1977), 245–250.

9. Dana, *Two Years Before the Mast,* 59–60, 135–136; A. Robinson, *Life in California,* 51; David J. Weber, "'Scarce more than apes': Historical Roots of Anglo-American Stereotypes of Mexicans," in Weber, ed., *New Spain's Far Northern Frontier* (Albuquerque: University of New Mexico Press, 1979), 295. Refer also to C. Robinson, *Mexico and the Hispanic Southwest in American Literature,* 72–75.

10. William A. Streeter, "Recollections of Historical Events in California, 1843–1878" (Bancroft Library, ms., University of California, Berkeley); Pitt, *Decline of the Californios,* 19–20; Walton Bean, *California — An Interpretive History* (New York: McGraw-Hill, 1968), 95–98.

11. For the "Polk-Stockton conspiracy" interpretation of the war, see Glen Price, *Origins of the War with Mexico: The Polk-Stockton Intrigue* (Austin: University of Texas Press, 1967). For the Bear Flag Revolt and its effect on Mexicans, see Rodolfo Acuña, *Occupied America: A History of Chicanos* (2nd ed., New York: Harper & Row, 1981), 96–97.

12. Neal Harlow, *California Conquered* (Berkeley and Los Angeles: University of California Press, 1982), chaps. 9 through 14.

13. David J. Weber, *Foreigners in Their Native Land: Historical Roots of the Mexican Americans* (Albuquerque: University of New Mexico Press, 1973), 140–144.

CHAPTER TWO

1. Quoted in Robert G. Cleland, *The Cattle on a Thousand Hills* (San Marino, Calif.: Huntington Library, 1951), 41.

2. *Ibid.*, 43.

3. Leonard Pitt, *The Decline of the Californios: A Social History of the Spanish-Speaking Californians, 1846–1890* (Berkeley and Los Angeles: University of California Press, 1966), 83–103.

4. For accounts of Murieta and Vásquez, see Pedro Castillo and Albert Camarillo, eds., *Furia y Muerte: Los Bandidos Chicanos* (Los Angeles: UCLA Chicano Studies Center, Monograph No. 2, 1973).

5. *Los Angeles Star*, 16 May 1874, quoted in Cleland, *Cattle on a Thousand Hills*, 274.

6. Pitt, *Decline of the Californios*, 148–180; Albert Camarillo, *Chicanos in a Changing Society: From Mexican Pueblos to American Barrios in Santa Barbara and Southern California, 1846–1930* (Cambridge: Harvard University Press, 1979), 18–22; Hubert H. Bancroft, *California Pastoral, 1769–1848* (San Francisco: The History Co., 1888).

7. Camarillo, *Chicanos in a Changing Society*, 15; Pitt, *Decline of the Californios*, 167.

8. Richard Griswold del Castillo, *The Los Angeles Barrio, 1850–1890* (Berkeley and Los Angeles: University of California Press, 1979), 160. See also Mario García, "The Californios of San Diego and the Politics of Accommodation," *Aztlán*, VI (Spring 1975), 70–72, 79–80; Ray A. Billington and Albert Camarillo, *The American Southwest: Myth and Reality* (Los Angeles: UCLA Clark Memorial Library, 1979), 43–47.

9. Camarillo, *Chicanos in a Changing Society*, 71–76.

10. *Ibid.*, 76.

11. Pitt, *Decline of the Californios*, 107–108; Camarillo, *Chicanos in a Changing Society*, 36.

12. Dario Oreña, *Reminiscences of Early California* (typescript, Santa Barbara Historical Society, 1932), 57; see also, Camarillo, *Chicanos in a Changing Society*, 11–13.

13. Mario Barrera, *Race and Class in the Southwest* (Notre Dame, Ind.: University of Notre Dame Press, 1979), 19–20.

14. David Hornbeck, *California Patterns: A Geographical and Historical Atlas* (Palo Alto, Calif.: Mayfield, 1983), 68.

15. Antonia I. Castañeda, "The Impact of the Conquest and Economic Transformation: Occupational Stratification and Mexicanos in Monterey and Santa Cruz, 1836–1870," paper presented at the Western History Association meeting (San Diego, October 1979); Antonio R. Soto, "The Chicano and the Church in Northern California, 1848–1978: A Study of an Ethnic Minority within the Roman Catholic Church" (Ph.D. dissertation, University of California, Berkeley, 1978), 88; *Transactions of the American Institute of Mining Engineers, 13, Feb. 1884 to June 1885* (New York: Institute of Mining Engineers, 1885), 182–185; George J. Sánchez, "Adaptation to Conquest: The Mexican Community of San Jose, 1845–1880" (unpublished paper, Stanford University, 1982).

16. For a description of the tourist–real estate booms, see Glenn S. Dumke, *The Boom of the Eighties in Southern California* (San Marino, Calif.: Huntington Library, 1955).

17. "SM's Original Families Suffer Discrimination," *Santa Monica Evening Outlook*, 17 May 1975; see also Camarillo, *Chicanos in a Changing Society*, 54–65, 117–126.

18. For Los Angeles organizations, see Griswold del Castillo, *Los Angeles Barrio*, 134–138; for the Spanish-American Independent Political Club of San Francisco, see *San Diego Daily Union*, 3 April 1874.

19. Michael C. Neri, "A Journalistic Portrait of the Spanish-Speaking People of California, 1868–1925," *Historical Society Quarterly of Southern California*, LV (Summer 1973), 197.

20. Camarillo, *Chicanos in a Changing Society*, 126–139; Castañeda, "Impact of Conquest," 30–38; Antonio R. Soto, "Chicano Reaction to Social Change in Northern California, 1848–1908," paper presented at the National Association of Chicano Social Science meeting (Berkeley, April 1977), 23–25.

21. Juan Caballeria, *History of San Bernardino Valley: From the Padres to the Pioneers, 1810–1851* (San Bernardino, Calif.: Times-Index Press, 1902), 212.

CHAPTER THREE

1. Among the best sources for analyzing Mexican immigration to California and the U.S. for this period are Lawrence Cardoso, *Mexican Emigration to the United States, 1897–1931* (Tucson: University of Arizona Press, 1980) and Manuel Gamio, *Mexican Immigration to the United States: A Study of Human Migration and Adjustment* (Chicago: University of Chicago Press, 1930). Quotes are taken from Manuel

Gamio, *The Life Story of the Mexican Immigrant* (Chicago: University of Chicago Press, 1930; reprinted New York: Dover Publications, 1971), 2–3.

2. *Mexicans in California*, Report of Governor C. C. Young's Mexican Fact-Finding Committee (San Francisco: California State Printing Office, 1930; reprinted San Francisco: R and E Research Associates, 1970), 31.

3. Mario Barrera, *Race and Class in the Southwest* (Notre Dame, Ind.: University of Notre Dame Press, 1979), 76–93.

4. Quote from Paul S. Taylor, *Mexican Labor in the United States* (7 vols., Berkeley: University of California Press, 1930), I, 40, 18; *Mexicans in California*, 79–91; Barrera, *Race and Class*, 76–91.

5. Ernesto Galarza, *Barrio Boy* (Notre Dame, Ind.: University of Notre Dame Press, 1971), 194–196.

6. For sources on demographic distribution of the Mexican population between 1915 and 1930, see *Mexicans in California*, 43–59. See also, Camarillo, *Chicanos in a Changing Society*, 200–201; Taylor, *Mexican Labor*, I, 81–83.

7. For examples of mutualistas and other organizations in California's Mexican American communities see Taylor, *Mexican Labor*, I, 62–64; Ricardo Romo, *East Los Angeles — History of a Barrio* (Austin: University of Texas Press, 1983), 142–154; Camarillo, *Chicanos in a Changing Society*, 147–154; Gamio, *Mexican Immigration*, 242–244; José A. Hernández, *Mutual Aid for Survival: The Case of the Mexican American* (Malabar, Fla.: Robert E. Krieger, 1983), 75–84.

8. Gamio, *Life Story*, 21–25, 87–92.

9. Paul S. Taylor, "Mexican Women in Los Angeles Industry in 1928," *Aztlán*, XI (Spring 1980), 102–114; *Mexicans in California*, 77–95; Ricardo Romo, "Work and Restlessness: Occupational and Spatial Mobility among Mexicans in Los Angeles, 1918–1928," *Pacific Historical Review*, XLVI (May 1977), 157–180; Camarillo, *Chicanos in a Changing Society*, 210–225. For Mexican women in the food processing industry, see Vicki L. Ruiz, "UCAPAWA, Chicanas, and the California Food Processing Industry, 1937–1950" (unpublished dissertation, Stanford University, 1982).

10. Juan Gómez-Quiñones, "The First Steps: Chicano Labor Conflict and Organizing, 1900–1920," *Aztlán*, III (Spring 1972), 25–31; Rodolfo Acuña, *Occupied America: A History of Chicanos* (2nd ed., New York: Harper & Row, 1981), 199–200, 211–213. See also Tomás

Almaguer and Albert Camarillo, "Urban Chicano Workers in Historical Perspective: A Review of Recent Literature," in Armando Valdez *et al.*, eds., *Work, Family, and Migration in Chicano Research* (Stanford, Calif.: Stanford Center for Chicano Research, 1982).

11. Charles Wollenberg, "Working on El Traque: The Pacific Electric Strike of 1903," in Norris Hundley, ed., *The Chicano* (Santa Barbara, Calif.: Clio Books, 1975), 96–107 ; Camarillo, *Chicanos in a Changing Society*, 170–171.

12. Taylor, *Mexican Labor*, 75–79, 258–275 ; quotes are from Charles Wollenberg, *All Deliberate Speed: Segregation and Exclusion in California Public Schools, 1855–1975* (Berkeley and Los Angeles: University of California Press, 1976), 111, 118.

13. Romo, *East Los Angeles*, 130–144 ; Camarillo, *Chicanos in a Changing Society*, 161–163, 225–227.

14. For immigration restriction and early deportation, see Abraham Hoffman, *Unwanted Mexican Americans in the Great Depression: Repatriation Pressures, 1929–1939* (Tucson: University of Arizona Press, 1974); Ricardo Romo, "Responses to Mexican Immigration, 1910–1930," *Aztlán*, VI (Summer 1975), 173–194 ; Acuña, *Occupied America*, 128–142.

15. *Mexicans in California*, 95, 171.

CHAPTER FOUR

1. Ricardo Romo, *East Los Angeles—History of a Barrio* (Austin: University of Texas Press, 1983), 162.

2. Quotes from George Kiser and David Silverman, "Mexican Repatriation during the Great Depression," in George C. Kiser and Martha W. Kiser, eds., *Mexican Workers in the United States* (Albuquerque: University of New Mexico Press, 1979), 56–58. Abraham Hoffman's *Unwanted Mexican Americans in the Great Depression: Repatriation Pressures, 1929–1939* (Tucson: University of Arizona Press, 1974) is still the only book-length study on the topic; it focuses on the Los Angeles deportation drive. See also Albert Camarillo, *Chicanos in a Changing Society: From Mexican Pueblos to American Barrios in Santa Barbara and Southern California, 1846–1930* (Cambridge: Harvard University Press, 1979), 162–163.

3. Francisco Balderrama, *In Defense of La Raza: The Los Angeles Mexican Consulate and the Mexican Community, 1929–1936* (Tucson: University of Arizona Press, 1982), 18–19. See also Rodolfo Acuña, *Occupied*

America: A History of Chicanos (2nd ed., NewYork: Harper & Row, 1981), 138–142; Emory Bogardus, *The Mexican in the United States* (Los Angeles: University of Southern California Press, 1934; New York: Arno Press, 1970), 94–95.

4. Bogardus, *The Mexican in the United States*, 94.

5. Luis Valdez and Stan Steiner, *Aztlán—An Anthology of Mexican American Literature* (NewYork: Vintage Books, 1972), 135.

6. The quotes, as they appear in order, are cited in the following: Camarillo, *Chicanos in a Changing Society*, 163; Carey McWilliams, *North from Mexico: The Spanish-Speaking People of the United States* (1948; New York: Greenwood Press, 1968), 193; Balderrama, *In Defense of La Raza*, 28.

7. Balderrama, *In Defense of La Raza*, 28.

8. *Ibid.*, chaps. 2 and 3.

9. For a good overview of California farm labor and conflict during the 1930s, see Sam Kushner, *The Long Road to Delano* (New York: International Publishers, 1974); Carey McWilliams, *Factories in the Fields: The Story of Migratory Labor in California* (1944; Santa Barbara, Calif.: Peregrine Publishers, 1971); Dick Meister and Ann Loftis, *A Long Time Coming: The Struggle to Unionize American Farm Workers* (New York: Macmillan, 1977); Cletus E. Daniel, *Bitter Harvest—A History of California Farmworkers 1870–1941* (Berkeley and Los Angeles: University of California Press, 1982).

10. Ronald López, "The El Monte Berry Strike," *Aztlán*, I (Spring 1970), 101–111; Acuña, *Occupied America*, 219–221.

11. Kushner, *Long Road to Delano*, 86–87; McWilliams, *North from Mexico*, 191–192.

12. Vicki L. Ruiz, "UCAPAWA, Chicanas, and the California Food Processing Industry, 1937–1950" (unpublished dissertation, Stanford University, 1982); Victor Nelson-Cisneros, "UCAPAWA in California: The Farm Worker Period," *Aztlán*, VII (Fall 1976), 453–478.

13. Clementina Durón, "Mexican Women and Labor Conflict in Los Angeles: The ILGWU Dressmakers' Strike of 1933," *Aztlán* (forthcoming); Douglas Munroy, "Las Costura en Los Angeles, 1933–1939: The ILGWU and the Politics of Domination," in Magdalena Mora and Adelaida R. del Castillo, eds., *Mexican Women in the United States: Struggles Past and Present* (Los Angeles: Chicano Studies Research Center Publications, University of California, Los Angeles, 1980). For other urban labor strife in Los Angeles, see Luis L.

Arroyo, "Chicano Participation in Organized Labor: The CIO in Los Angeles, 1938–1950. An Extended Research Note," *Aztlán,* VI (Summer 1975), 227–303.

14. Interviews with Luisa Moreno by Albert Camarillo, 1976 and 1977, and by Vicki Ruiz, 1979; interview with Bert Corona by Albert Camarillo, 1977. See also Acuña, *Occupied America,* 317–318.

15. Interview with Bert Corona (1977).

16. First National Congress, "Digest of Proceedings," file M224, Ernesto Galarza Papers, Department of Special Collections, Stanford University; interviews by Albert Camarillo with Josephine Fierro de Bright, hereafter referred to only as Fierro, (1977), Luisa Moreno (1976 and 1977), and Bert Corona (1977); *La Opinión,* 27 and 30 April 1939; *UCAPAWA News,* July 1939; and *People's World,* 28 and 30 April, 1939.

17. See file M322, Manuel Ruiz, Jr., Papers, Department of Special Collections, Stanford University; interviews with Fierro (1977), Moreno (1976 and 1977), and Corona (1977).

18. See file M295, Ruiz Papers; see also Acuña, *Occupied America,* 316–317.

19. For discussion of the interpretations about pachucos, see Arturo Madrid-Barela, "In Search of the Authentic Pachuco," *Aztlán,* IV (Spring 1973), 31–60.

20. McWilliams, *North from Mexico,* 229–231.

21. *Ibid.,* 231–232; interviews with Fierro (1977) and Moreno (1976).

22. Interview with Fierro (1977).

23. McWilliams, *North from Mexico,* 244–255; Acuña, *Occupied America,* 326–329. A different interpretation of the motivations of servicemen involved in the riots is presented in Mauricio Mazón, *The Zoot Suit Riots: The Psychology of Symbolic Annihilation* (Austin: University of Texas Press, 1984).

24. *Esquire,* May 1983, 50.

CHAPTER FIVE

1. Leonel Apodaca, "A Study of Mexican Immigrants in San Jose," (unpublished paper, Stanford University, 1977).

2. Raul Morín, *Among the Valiant: Mexican Americans in W W II and Korea* (Alhambra, Calif.: Borden, 1966), 91, 112.

3. Interview with Larry Amaya (1971); Morín, *Among the Valiant,* 112.

4. Morín, *Among the Valiant,* 27–33.

5. Rodolfo Acuña, *Occupied America: A History of Chicanos* (2nd ed., New York: Harper & Row, 1981), 323.

6. Morín, *Among the Valiant,* 59–74, 254–255; interview with Larry Amaya.

7. Leo Grebler, Joan Moore, and Ralph Guzmán, *The Mexican-American People: The Nation's Second Largest Minority* (New York: Free Press, 1970), 217; Albert Camarillo, "Chicano Urban History: a Study of Compton's Barrio, 1936–1970," *Aztlán,* II (Fall 1972), 91, 102–103; Mario Barrera, *Race and Class in the Southwest* (Notre Dame, Ind.: University of Notre Dame Press, 1979), 140–141.

8. Interviews with Luisa Moreno (1977), Josephine Fierro (1977), and Bert Corona (1971 and 1977); Luis L. Arroyo, "Chicano Participation in Organized Labor: The CIO in Los Angeles, 1938–1950. An Extended Research Note," *Aztlán,* VI (Summer 1975), 280–297.

9. For the best studies on the bracero program, see Ernesto Galarza, *Merchants of Labor* (Charlotte, N.C.: McNally & Loftin, 1964); and Richard Craig, *The Bracero Program: Interest Groups and Foreign Policy* (Austin: University of Texas Press, 1971).

10. David G. Pfeiffer, "The Bracero Program in Mexico," in George C. Kiser and Martha W. Kiser, eds., *Mexican Workers in the United States* (Albuquerque: University of New Mexico Press, 1979), 71–84; Acuña, *Occupied America,* 144–150.

11. Albert Camarillo, *Chicanos in a Changing Society: From Mexican Pueblos to American Barrios in Santa Barbara and Southern California, 1846–1930* (Cambridge: Harvard University Press, 1979), 255; Ricardo Romo, "The Urbanization of Southwestern Chicanos in the Early 20th Century," *New Scholar,* VI (1977), 194.

12. Marta Tienda, "Residential Distribution and Internal Migration Patterns of Chicanos: A Critical Assessment," in Armando Valdez *et al., The State of Chicano Research in Family, Labor, and Migration Studies* (Stanford, Calif.: Stanford Center for Chicano Research, 1983), 154. For rural-to-urban migration and urbanization, see also Grebler *et al., Mexican-American People,* 105–111; Clark Knowlton, "Changing Spanish-American Villages of Northern New Mexico," *Sociology and Social Research,* V (1969), 464. For sources that address the effects of assimilation, see Manual Gamio, *The Life Story of the Mexican Immigrant* (1930; New York: Dover Publications, 1970); Paul S. Taylor,

"Mexican Women in Los Angeles Industry in 1928," *Aztlán*, XI (Spring 1980), 102–114; Emory Bogardus, *The Mexican in the United States* (1934; New York: Arno Press, 1970); Grebler *et al.*, *Mexican-American People*, 196–206, 405–408.

13. Maria Morena, "I'm Talking Justice," in Magdalena Mora and Adelaida R. del Castillo, *Mexican Women in the United States: Struggles Past and Present* (Los Angeles: Chicano Studies Research Center Publications, University of California, Los Angeles 1980), 181. See also Grebler *et al.*, *Mexican-American People*, 107–109; Elizabeth Broadbent, "Mexican Population in the Southwestern United States," *Texas Geographic Magazine*, V (1941), 727–737.

14. Grebler *et al.*, *Mexican-American People*, 112–115.

15. Morín, *Among the Valiant*, 277–278.

16. Vesta Penrod, "Civil Rights Problems of Mexican-Americans in Southern California," (M.A. thesis, Claremont Graduate School, 1948); Carey McWilliams, *North from Mexico: The Spanish-Speaking People of the United States* (1948; New York: Greenwood Press, 1968), 280–284; Ruth D. Tuck, *Not With the Fist* (New York: Harcourt, Brace, 1946), 161.

17. Quoted in Alonso S. Perales, *Are We Good Neighbors?* (1948; New York: Arno Press, 1974), 81.

18. Morín, *Among the Valiant*, 278.

19. Miguel Tirado, "Mexican American Community Political Organization, the Key to Chicano Political Power," *Aztlán*, I (Spring 1970), 61–62; Penrod, "Civil Rights Problems," 27–29; Acuña, *Occupied America*, 330–332.

20. Interviews with Anthony Ríos, founding member and past president of CSO (1970 and 1971); *20th Anniversary of the Los Angeles Community Service Organization* (25 March 1967); *Los Angeles Free Press*, 1 March 1956; Tirado, "Mexican American Community Political Organization," 62–64.

21. Charles Wollenberg, *All Deliberate Speed: Segregation and Exclusion in California Public Schools, 1855–1975* (Berkeley and Los Angeles: University of California Press, 1976), 108–135.

22. *Ibid.*, 134; Grebler *et al.*, *Mexican-American People*, 190.

23. Acuña, *Occupied America*, 156; Julian Samora, *Los Mojados: The Wetback Story* (Notre Dame, Ind.: University of Notre Dame Press, 1971), 51–55.

CHAPTER SIX

1. Wilson Craig, "The Mexican American Political Association in California," (M.A. thesis, Sonoma State College, 1970), 26–54; Armando Gutiérrez, "The Evolution of Chicano Politics," *Aztlán,* V (Spring and Fall 1974), 69–70; Miguel Tirado, "Mexican American Community Political Organization, the Key to Chicano Political Power," *Aztlán,* I (Spring 1970), 66–68.

2. For a discussion of farm labor prior to 1960, see Ernesto Galarza, *Farm Workers and Agri-Business in California, 1947–1980* (Notre Dame, Ind.: University of Notre Dame Press, 1977) and *Spiders in the House—Workers in the Field* (Notre Dame, Ind.: University of Notre Dame Press, 1970).

3. The history of the UFW and Chávez are aptly covered in Ronald B. Taylor, *Chavez and the Farm Workers* (Boston: Beacon Press, 1975) and Peter Matthiessen, *Sal Si Puedes: Cesar Chavez and the New American Revolution* (New York: Random House, 1969).

4. U.S. Bureau of the Census, *Census of Population, 1960,* vol. I (Washington, D.C.: U.S. Government Printing Office, 1963); Bureau of the Census, *Persons of Spanish Origin in the United States: November 1969,* Current Population Reports (Washington, D.C.: U.S. Government Printing Office, 1971); Paul Sheldon, "Mexican Americans in Urban Public Schools: An Exploration of the Dropout Problem," *California Journal of Education Research,* XII (January 1961); Leo Grebler, Joan Moore, and Ralph Guzmán, *The Mexican-American People: The Nation's Second Largest Minority* (New York: Free Press, 1970), 143, 197, 208, 252.

5. For aspects of the Chicano movement during the late 1960s, see the following: Gerald Rosen, "The Development of the Chicano Movement in Los Angeles from 1967 to 1969," *Aztlán,* IV (Spring 1973), 155–174; Joan Moore with Alfredo Cuellar, *Mexican-Americans* (Englewood Cliffs, N.J.: Prentice-Hall, 1970), 148–153; Gutiérrez, "Evolution of Chicano Politics," 78–82.

6. Tomás Ybarra-Frausto, *Califas: Chicano Art and Its Social Background* (Mary Porter Sesnon Gallery, University of California, Santa Cruz, forthcoming); Jacinto Quirate, *Mexican American Art and Artists* (Austin: University of Texas Press, 1973).

7. For brief descriptions of some community service and political organizations, see Matt S. Meier and Feliciano Rivera, *Dictionary of Mexican American History* (Westport, Conn.: Greenwood Press, 1981);

Rodolfo Acuña, *Occupied America: A History of Chicanos* (2nd ed., New York: Harper & Row, 1981), ch. 11.

8. Christine Sierra, "Political Transformation of a Minority Organization: The Council of La Raza, 1965–1980" (Ph.D. dissertation, Stanford University, 1982) is the first in-depth study of the National Council of La Raza.

9. For LRUP, see Richard Santillan, *Chicano Politics: La Raza Unida* (Los Angeles: Tlaquila Publishers, 1973); Gutiérrez, "Evolution of Chicano Politics," 76–77; John S. Shockley, *Chicano Revolt in a Texas Town* (Notre Dame, Ind.: University of Notre Dame Press, 1974).

10. Ralph Guzmán, "Mexican-American Casualties in Vietnam," *La Raza*, I, cited in Acuña, *Occupied America*, 366–367; see also Alejandro Morales, *Ando Sangrando—I Am Bleeding: A Study of Mexican American–Police Conflict* (La Puente, Calif.: Perspectiva Publications, 1972), 91–122.

11. David Gutiérrez, "CASA in the Chicano Movement: A Study of Organizational Politics and Ideology in the Chicano Movement, 1968–1978" (unpublished paper, Stanford University, 1982).

12. Helen S. Astin and Cecilia P. Burciaga, *Chicanos in Higher Education: Progress and Attainment* (Los Angeles: Higher Education Research Institute, 1981), 32.

13. Carlos Muñoz, Jr., "The Politics of Protest and Chicano Liberation: A Case Study of Repression and Cooptation," *Aztlán*, V (Spring and Fall 1974), 119–142; Gerald Rosen, "Development of the Chicano Movement," 159–160.

14. Juan Gómez-Quiñones, *Mexican Students por La Raza—The Chicano Student Movement in Southern California, 1967–1977* (Santa Barbara, Calif.: Editorial La Causa, 1978), 32. See also Carlos Muñoz, Jr., and Mario Barrera, "La Raza Unida Party and the Chicano Student Movement," *Social Science Journal*, XIX (1982), 101–119.

15. For the Chicana movement, see Adaliza Sosa Riddell, "Chicanas and el Movimiento," *Aztlán*, V (Spring and Fall 1974), 155–166; Magdalena Mora and Adelaida R. del Castillo, *Mexican Women in the United States: Struggles Past and Present* (Los Angeles: Chicano Studies Research Center, University of California, Los Angeles, 1980), 1–61; Martha P. Cotera, *The Chicana Feminist* (Austin, Tex.: Information Systems Development, 1977); Alfredo Mirandé and Evangelina Enríquez, *La Chicana—The Mexican American Woman* (Chicago: University of Chicago Press, 1980).

16. For the few studies that discuss the relationship between Chicanos and the church, see Antonio R. Soto, "The Chicano and the Church in Northern California, 1848–1978" (Ph.D. dissertation, University of California, Berkeley, 1978); César Chávez, "The Mexican American and the Church," *El Grito,* IV (Summer 1968), 9–12; Acuña, *Occupied America,* 405–408.

17. Carlos E. Cortés, "Mexicans," in Stephan Thernstrom, ed., *Harvard Encyclopedia of American Ethnic Groups* (Cambridge: Harvard University Press, 1980), 719.

EPILOGUE

1. U.S. Bureau of the Census, Supplementary Report, PC80-S1-7, *Persons of Spanish Origin by State: 1980* (Washington, D.C.: U.S. Government Printing Office, August 1982), 6, 12.

2. "Spanish Origin Population Change in Selected California Counties 1960, 1970, and 1980" (Stanford, Calif.: Stanford Center for Chicano Research, 1983); *Projections of the Hispanic Population for the United States 1990 and 2000* (Palo Alto, Calif.: Center for the Continuing Study of the California Economy, 1982), 26, 29.

3. *Projections of the Hispanic Population,* 33.

4. For a discussion of the estimates of the numbers of undocumented Mexicans in the U.S. during the 1970s, see the following: Manuel García y Griego and Leonardo F. Estrada, "Research on the Magnitude of Mexican Undocumented Immigration to the U.S.: A Summary," in Antonio Ríos-Bustamante, ed., *Mexican Immigrant Workers in the U.S.* (Los Angeles: Chicano Studies Research Center, University of California, Los Angeles, 1981), 51–70; Dick J. Reavis, *Without Documents* (New York: Condor, 1978), 103–108; Harry B. Cross and James A. Sandos, *Across the Border: Rural Development in Mexico and Recent Migration to the United States* (Berkeley: Institute of Governmental Studies, University of California, Berkeley, 1981), 81–84, 150–152.

5. Thomas Muller, *The Fourth Wave: California's Newest Immigrants — A Summary* (Washington, D.C.: Urban Institute, 1983), 5–6.

6. *Racial and Ethnic Distribution of Students and Staff in California Public Schools: Fall 1981* (Sacramento: California State Department of Education, 1981): Stephen L. Daigle, *Ethnic Data and Higher Education — A Reference Guide for the California State University* (Long Beach: California State University, Office of the Chancellor, Student Affirmative Action Unit, May 1983), sections 3-5, 3-8, and 3-11.

7. *Ethnic Data and Higher Education,* section 3-19; see also Alexander Astin, *Minorities in Higher Education: Recent Trends, Current Prospects, and Recommendations* (San Francisco: Jossey-Bass, 1982), 27; *Racial and Ethnic Distribution of Students and Staff in California Public Schools* (Sacramento: California State Department of Education, Office of Intergroup Relations, Fall 1979); Helen Astin and Cecilia P. Burciaga, *Chicanos in Higher Education: Progress and Attainment* (Los Angeles: Higher Education Research Institute, November 1981), 23-26.

8. *California Labor Market Issues: Hispanics* (Sacramento: State of California Health and Welfare Agency, Employment Development Department, September 1981), 10-11.

9. Based on data from *Current Population Survey of California, 1978,* cited in *California Labor Market Issues,* 4-43.

10. *Ibid.,* 15-20.

11. *Ibid.,* 15.

12. See, for example, the following: "The Decade of the Chicano," *New West,* 11 September 1978; "Hispanic Americans," *Time,* 16 October 1978, 48-61; "Hispanics Make Their Move," *U.S. News and World Report,* 24 August 1981.

SUGGESTED READINGS

AMONG GENERAL WORKS, an excellent overview essay on
Mexican Americans was written by Carlos E. Cortés,
"Mexicans," in Stephan Thernstrom, ed., *Harvard Encyclopedia
of American Ethnic Groups* (Cambridge: Harvard University Press,
1980). The writings of Carey McWilliams are still central for
understanding the development of themes in Chicano history,
particularly his *Southern California Country: An Island on the
Land* (New York: Duell, Sloan & Pearce, 1946) and, most importantly, *North from Mexico: The Spanish-Speaking People of the
United States* (1948; New York: Greenwood Press ed., 1968).
Other general histories of note include Rodolfo Acuña, *Occupied
America: A History of Chicanos* (2nd ed., New York: Harper &
Row, 1981) and Matt S. Meier and Feliciano Rivera, *The Chicanos* (New York: Hill & Wang, 1972). Three articles which
survey the literature on Mexican American history up to 1974
are Juan Gómez-Quiñones and Luis L. Arroyo, "On the State of
Chicano History: Observations on Its Development, Interpreta-
tions, and Theory, 1970-1974," *Western Historical Quarterly,* VII
(April 1976):155-185; Arthur Corwin, "Mexican-American
History: An Assessment," *Pacific Historical Review,* XLII (August
1973): 269-308; Juan Gómez-Quiñones, "Toward a Perspective on Chicano History," *Aztlán: Chicano Journal of the Social
Sciences and the Arts,* III (Spring 1972), 13-49. Recent essays
reviewing the historical and social science literature on Mexican
American families, employment, and migration were published
in Armando Valdez *et al., The State of Chicano Research in Family,
Labor, and Migration Studies* (Stanford: Stanford Center for Chicano Research, Stanford University, 1983). Mario Barrera's *Race
and Class in the Southwest* (Notre Dame, Ind.: University of
Notre Dame Press, 1979) is also useful as a theoretical and
historical overview of the Mexican American working class.

For the nineteenth century, the following books treat various topics. The demise of cattle ranching and the impact on Mexican rancheros is documented well by Leonard Pitt, *The Decline of the Californios: A Social History of the Spanish-Speaking Californians, 1846–1890* (Berkeley and Los Angeles: University of California Press, 1966). The transformation of specific Mexican communities during the half century after the Mexican-American war is the topic of books by Richard Griswold del Castillo, *The Los Angeles Barrio, 1850–1890* (Berkeley and Los Angeles: University of California Press, 1979) and Albert Camarillo, *Chicanos in a Changing Society: From Mexican Pueblos to American Barrios in Santa Barbara and Southern California, 1848–1930* (Cambridge: Harvard University Press, 1979). Other useful studies of Mexican Americans in California and the Southwest during the 1800s include David J. Weber, *Foreigners in Their Native Land: Historical Roots of the Mexican Americans* (Albuquerque: University of New Mexico Press, 1973) and Cecil Robinson, *Mexico and the Hispanic Southwest in American Literature* (Tucson: University of Arizona Press, 1977). Reprinted essays on the "bandits" Joaquín Murieta and Tiburcio Vásquez were published in Pedro Castillo and Albert Camarillo, eds., *Furia y Muerte: Los Bandidos Chicanos* (Los Angeles: Aztlán Publications, Monograph No. 2, Chicano Studies Center, University of California, Los Angeles, 1973).

For the early twentieth century, especially on the topic of Mexican immigrants, the classic works of Manuel Gamio and Paul S. Taylor should be consulted: Manuel Gamio, *Mexican Immigration to the United States: A Study of Human Migration and Adjustment* (1930; New York: Dover Publications, 1971); Paul S. Taylor, *Mexican Labor in the United States* (7 vols., Berkeley: University of California Press, 1930–1932). Recent urban barrio case studies for the period up to the Great Depression include Ricardo Romo, *East Los Angeles—History of a Barrio* (Austin: University of Texas Press, 1983) and Albert Camarillo, *Chicanos in a Changing Society.*

Studies that deal with Mexicans during the Great Depression and World War II include Abraham Hoffman, *Unwanted Mexican Americans in the Great Depression: Repatriation Pressures, 1929–1939* (Tucson: University of Arizona Press, 1974); Francisco Balderrama, *In Defense of La Raza: The Los Angeles Mexican Consulate and the Mexican Community* (Tucson: University of Arizona

Press, 1982); Ruth Tuck, *Not With the Fist* (New York: Harcourt, Brace, 1946); Raul Morín, *Among the Valiant: Mexican Americans in W W II and Korea* (Alhambra, Calif.: Borden, 1966); Mauricio Mazón, *The Zoot Suit Riots: The Psychology of Symbolic Annihilation* (Austin: University of Texas Press, 1984).

Dozens of books have been published on California farm workers, on César Chávez, and on the Bracero Program. Ernesto Galarza contributed three outstanding volumes: *Farm Workers and Agri-Business in California, 1947–1960* (Notre Dame, Ind.: University of Notre Dame Press, 1977), *Spiders in the House — Workers in the Field* (Notre Dame, Ind.: University of Notre Dame Press, 1970), and *Merchants of Labor* (Charlotte, N.C.: McNally & Loftin, 1964). Farm labor history is also covered by Sam Kushner, *The Long Road to Delano* (New York: International Publishers, 1975); Cletus E. Daniel, *Bitter Harvest — A History of California Farmworkers, 1870–1941* (Berkeley and Los Angeles: University of California Press, 1982); Dick Meister and Ann Loftis, *A Long Time Coming: The Struggle to Unionize American Farm Workers* (New York: Macmillan, 1977). In addition to most of the books noted above which mention Chávez and the UFW, the studies by Jacques Levy, *Cesar Chavez: Autobiography of La Causa* (New York: W. W. Norton, 1975) and Ronald B. Taylor, *Chavez and the Farm Workers* (Boston: Beacon Press, 1975) are most informative.

Several novels and autobiographies provide literary perspectives on many Chicano historical themes in California. The autobiography of Ernesto Galarza, *Barrio Boy* (Notre Dame, Ind.: University of Notre Dame Press, 1971) and the novel by José Antonio Villarreal, *Pocho* (New York: Doubleday, 1959) portray themes of immigrant adjustment, cultural conflict, and assimilation. Other novels focusing on Mexican Americans in California include Raymond Barrio, *The Plum Plum Pickers* (Sunnyvale, Calif.: Ventura Press, 1969); Richard Vásquez, *Chicano* (New York: Avon, 1970); Oscar Zeta Acosta, *The Autobiography of a Brown Buffalo* (San Francisco: Straight Arrow Books, 1972) and *Revolt of the Cockroach People* (San Francisco: Straight Arrow Books, 1973).

Studies which have valuable general information concerning education, occupation, and other socioeconomic variables include Leo Grebler, Joan Moore, and Ralph Guzmán, *The Mexican*

American People: The Nation's Second Largest Minority (New York: Free Press, 1970); Thomas P. Carter, *Mexican Americans in School: A History of Educational Neglect* (New York: College Entrance Examination Board, 1970); Helen S. Astin and Cecilia Burciaga, *Chicanos in Higher Education: Progress and Attainment* (Los Angeles: Higher Education Research Institute, 1981); *California Labor Market Issues: Hispanics* (Sacramento: State of California Health and Welfare Agency, Employment Development Department, September 1981); Fred Romero, *Chicano Workers: Their Utilization and Development* (Los Angeles: Chicano Studies Research Center, University of California, Los Angeles, 1979).

Useful collections of readings on Mexican American women may be found in Magdalena Mora and Adelaida R. del Castillo, eds., *Mexican Women in the United States: Struggles Past and Present* (Los Angeles: Chicano Studies Research Center, University of California, 1980); Rosaura Sánchez and Rosa Martínez Cruz, eds., *Essays on La Mujer* (Los Angeles: Chicano Studies Center Publications, University of California, Los Angeles, 1977); Margarita B. Melville, ed., *Twice a Minority: Mexican American Women* (St. Louis: C. V. Mosby, 1980). The only book length study on Chicanas is Alfredo Mirandé and Evangelina Enríquez, *La Chicana: The Mexican-American Woman* (Chicago: University of Chicago Press, 1979).

Few books are published that treat the Chicano movement of the 1960s. With the exception of the pamphlet by Juan Gómez-Quiñones, *Mexican Students por La Raza—The Chicano Student Movement in California, 1967–1977* (Santa Barbara, Calif.: Editorial La Causa, 1978), most publications are articles, some of which are cited in the notes to chapter five. Studies that deal with various aspects of contemporary Mexican American society include Alejandro Morales, *Ando Sangrando—I Am Bleeding: A Study of Mexican American–Police Conflict* (La Puente, Calif.: Perspective Publications, 1972); Joan W. Moore, *Homeboys—Gangs, Drugs, and Prison in the Barrios of Los Angeles* (Philadelphia: Temple University Press, 1978); Joseph Sommers and Tomás Ybarra-Frausto, eds., *Modern Chicano Writers: A Collection of Critical Essays* (Englewood Cliffs, N.J.: Prentice-Hall, 1979).

Humanities and social science literature on various themes and topics in Mexican American studies for the 1970s and 1980s are represented in the following collections of essays:

Isidro D. Ortiz, ed., *Chicanos and the Social Sciences: A Decade of Research and Development. Symposium Working Papers* (Santa Barbara, Calif.: Center for Chicano Studies, University of California, 1983); John A. García, ed., *The Chicano Struggle: Analyses of Past and Present Efforts* (New York: Bilingual Press, 1984); Carlos Vásquez and Manuel García y Griego, eds., *Mexican–U.S. Relations: Conflict and Convergence* (Los Angeles: Chicano Studies Research Center and Latin American Center, University of California, Los Angeles, 1983); Bruce-Novoa, *Chicano Authors: Inquiry by Interview* (Austin: University of Texas Press, 1980).

INDEX

Map (overleaf):
Refitted from and based on "Census Tracts–1980 Census": map by Western Economic Research Company. A full range of maps and reports are available from Western Economic Research Company, 15910 Ventura Blvd., Suite A-8, Encino, CA 91436.

Persons of Spa

San Fernando

South Pasade

Los Angeles

Vernon   Mo
                        Maywood
Huntington Park   Comme
              Bell

                                    Santa

Pacific Ocean

Wilmington

                                    Pacific Oc

© 1985 American Graphic Systems